To the precious iBreen, Addie.

About the Author

Christopher Breen has been writing about technology since the latter days of the Reagan administration for such publications as *MacUser, MacWEEK,* and *Macworld.* Currently a senior editor for *Macworld*, Breen pens its popular "Mac 911" tips-and-troubleshooting column and blog, routinely opines about digital media in its Playlist blog, and hosts the *Macworld Podcast.* He's the author of Peachpit's *The iPod & iTunes Pocket Guide, The iPhone Pocket Guide, The iPod touch Pocket Guide,* and *The Flip Mino Pocket Guide.* When not engaged in technological pursuits, he's a professional musician in the San Francisco Bay Area.

Acknowledgments

This book would be the fifth take on just another unrealized intriguing idea if not for the dedication of the following people.

At Peachpit Press: Publisher Nancy Ruenzel, who continues to support these efforts; Cliff Colby, who acceded to splitting the old iPod book into two books—one for "traditional" iPods and the other for the iPod touch; Kathy Simpson, who did everything that needed doing after the manuscript left my computer and took up residence on hers; production pro Myrna Vladic, who, with barely an anxious ripple, turned our work into the lovely book you hold now; David Van Ness, who made words and pictures fit so attractively within the confines of these pages; Debbie Roberti, who re-created the iPod's screens; and Rebecca Plunkett, who performed a book's most thankless yet necessary job: indexing.

At home: My wife, Claire, who manages to keep the house stocked with salt and cartridges, and who more than puts up with frantic nights and weekends of writing; and my daughter, Addie, who's getting so adept with these devices that she'll be able to take over the franchise one day.

Abroad: *Macworld* Editorial Director Jason Snell, who never said, "I'd like exclusive rights to that brain full of iPod goodness"; Terri Stone for the much-needed lunch breaks; Ben Long for his large and generous brain; and the boys from System 9 for their continued cool-cattedness.

And, of course, the designers, engineers, and other Apple folk who made the iPod and iTunes the phenomena they are. Congratulations!

The iPod & iTunes
PocketGuide
Fifth Edition

Christopher**Breen**

Ginormous knowledge, pocket-sized.

Peachpit
Press

The iPod & iTunes Pocket Guide, Fifth Edition
Christopher Breen

Peachpit Press
1249 Eighth Street
Berkeley, CA 94710
510/524-2178
510/524-2221 (fax)

Find us on the Web at: www.peachpit.com
To report errors, please send a note to errata@peachpit.com.

Peachpit Press is a division of Pearson Education.

Executive editor: Clifford Colby
Editor: Kathy Simpson
Production editor: Myrna Vladic
Compositor: David Van Ness
Illustrator: Debbie Roberti
Indexer: Rebecca Plunkett
Cover design: Peachpit Press
Cover image: Mike Tanamachi
Screen photo: iStockphoto
Interior design: Peachpit Press

ISBN-13: 978-0-321-64909-6
ISBN-10:   0-321-64909-5

9 8 7 6 5 4 3 2 1

Printed and bound in the United States of America

Contents

Getting Started

Though I admire your desire to learn more about the iPod by purchasing this little guide, my guess is that before you delve too deeply into this book, you'd like to actually use your iPod. That's what this chapter is for—getting you up and running as quickly as possible.

Here are the steps to take:

1. Look at the box.

   If the box tells you that you have an iPod touch, return this book for a copy of my *The iPod touch Pocket Guide* (Peachpit Press). The book you hold in your hands discusses the "traditional" iPod classic, iPod nano, and iPod shuffle only.

2. Open the box.

   After you've ripped the wrapping off your iPod, try turning it on. If it recently came from the factory, it could be charged and nearly ready to play.

3. Turn on the iPod.

   To switch on any display-bearing iPod, press and hold any of the buttons. (I have the best luck pressing the button in the center of the click wheel.) If the iPod is charged, it should display the Apple logo after a few seconds and be ready to roll in about 30 seconds.

> **tip** **If nothing happens when you try to start the iPod, make sure that the hold switch isn't on. (The hold switch is on the top of both of the latest iPod classics and the iPod nano.) If you see any orange next to the switch, the switch is on; slide it over to disengage it. If the iPod still won't start, it must be charged; see the "Charge It" sidebar.**

Charge It (If Necessary)

If the iPod doesn't work out of the box, you need to charge it up. On an iPod with a display (any iPod except the shuffle), you can do this by plugging the included USB cable into your computer's powered USB 2.0 port and plugging the other end of the cable into the bottom of the iPod. If you have a charger for your iPod (chargers are optional for all iPods), you can plug the cable's USB connector into the charger instead of your computer, plug the other end of the cable into your iPod, and plug the charger into a wall socket.

The iPod shuffle is charged from your computer's powered USB port via its included USB Dock (2G shuffle) or cable (3G shuffle). Plug the Dock or cable into a powered USB port to charge the shuffle.

For the iPod shuffle, push the power switch to the right. If a light (green or amber) glows on the LED next to the switch, the iPod is charged enough for you to play with it. If you don't see a light, the shuffle needs charging.

4. Listen to the radio (latest iPod nano only).

   If you have a fifth-generation (5G) iPod nano (see the sidebar "About This Generation Business"), you can listen to music on it right now as long as its battery is partially charged. Plug the included head-phones into the bottom of the nano, choose Radio in the main screen, and scroll your finger around the click wheel to tune in a local radio station.

About This Generation Business

Before I get too far into the ins and outs of the iPod and iTunes, let me define a convention that you'll see throughout this book. The iPod has been around for quite some time now, and in that time, there have been many iPod models—*generations* of iPod models, if you will. I occasionally refer to specific generations, and when I do, it's tiresome to write *third-generation* this and *fifth-generation* that. Instead, I refer to generations by using the capital letter *G*. So when you see, say, *3G*, know that I mean *third generation,* not *three giga-bytes* (which is abbreviated *3 GB*).

5. Install iTunes.

   If you don't already have a current copy of iTunes on your computer, download it from www.apple.com/itunes/download. (Apple hasn't bundled a CD copy of iTunes with the iPod for quite some time.) Follow whatever onscreen directions are necessary to put iTunes on your Windows PC or Mac.

6. Rip a CD.

No, don't actually rip the disc in half. *Rip* in this context means to transfer the audio from the CD to your computer. To do this, insert the disc into your computer's CD or DVD drive and then launch iTunes (if it doesn't launch automatically after you insert the disc). By default, iTunes 7 and later tosses up a dialog box that asks "Would you like to import the CD *NameofCD* into your iTunes library?" (where *NameofCD* is the name of your disc). Click Yes, and iTunes converts the audio files to a format that can be played on the iPod. Also, the tracks you ripped from the CD will appear in iTunes' main window when you click the Music entry in the iTunes Source list.

To import the CD at a later time, click No in this dialog box. Then, later, with that disc in the drive, select it in the Source list (it appears below the Devices heading), and click the Import CD button in the bottom-right corner of the iTunes window.

7. Plug in the iPod, if it's not plugged in already.

For an iPod other than a shuffle, this means stringing the included USB cable between a powered USB 2.0 port on the computer and the Dock-connector port on the bottom of the iPod. If you have a display-bearing iPod other than a nano, 5G iPod, 1G or 2G iPod classic, or any iPod touch, you can use a FireWire cable instead of the USB cable.

Today's 3G iPod shuffle uses a short USB cable that's included in the box. Plug the cylindrical end of the cable into the shuffle's headphone port and the USB connector into a free USB 2.0 port on your computer. The 2G iPod shuffles require the Dock that comes with them; just plug the Dock's cable into a free USB 2.0 port. Original iPod shuffle models (the ones that look like a fat stick of gum) have a built-in USB connector that plugs directly into your computer.

8. Register the iPod, and set up an iTunes account.

   After you plug in your iPod for the first time, a Welcome to Your New iPod window pops up, suggesting that you register your iPod and set up your iTunes Store account. Click Continue and agree to the license agreement, and you arrive at the iTunes Account (Apple ID) screen. In that screen, sign up for an account; enter the information for your existing account; or click Cancel. You'll be prompted to name your iPod and given the option to automatically sync songs and add photos (if your iPod can display photos).

   tip **If you're in a hurry to get something on your iPod, just click Register Later, agree to the license agreement, name your iPod, and click Done to continue.**

9. Get acquainted with iTunes.

   If your computer is connected to the Internet, the iTunes Store window automatically opens in the main iTunes window. Yes, Apple wants you to shop, but you don't have to right now.

   If you already have music in your iTunes Library, iTunes will ask you whether you'd like to import album artwork for your display-bearing iPod. Unless you have a dial-up connection to the Internet, let iTunes retrieve this artwork; it will make using your iPod and iTunes a more enjoyable experience (as you'll read later). If you have lots of tracks in your library—more than a few thousand—retrieving that artwork can take a while.

   iTunes will also seek out tracks that should be played gaplessly, such as music from albums like Pink Floyd's *Dark Side of the Moon* or any number of classical recordings in which one track should flow seamlessly into another.

   Although iTunes 7 and later can play music gaplessly, this feature is supported only on 5G and later full-size iPods (including the iPod touch and iPhone) and on 2G, 3G, 4G, and 5G iPod nanos. All earlier iPods play music with short gaps between tracks.

10. Transfer music to the iPod.

    By default, the iPod is configured so that it updates its music library automatically when it's connected to your computer. The music you ripped from your CD should transfer to the iPod quickly. If it doesn't, simply select your iPod in iTunes' Source list and choose File > Sync *Name of Your iPod* (where *Name of Your iPod* is . . . well, the name of your iPod).

11. Unmount and play.

    When the music has finished transferring, locate the name of your iPod in iTunes' Source list (it, too, appears below the Devices heading), and click the little Eject icon next to it. When the iPod disappears from iTunes, unplug it from your computer.

    Unwrap the earbuds that came with the iPod, jam them into your ears, and plug the other end into the iPod's headphone port. On an iPod with a click wheel on the front, rotate your thumb around the wheel until Shuffle Songs is selected; then press the iPod's Center button. On a 3G iPod shuffle, just switch the iPod on by sliding the power switch to the on position, plug in the included headphones, and press once in the center of the switch integrated into the right earbud's cord. If you have a 2G shuffle, switch the iPod on and press the large Play button.

    To adjust the volume on a click-wheel iPod, rotate your thumb clockwise to increase volume and counterclockwise to turn it down. On a 3G iPod shuffle, press the top of the headphone switch to turn the volume up. Press the bottom of the switch to decrease the volume. For a 2G iPod shuffle, press the plus (+) symbol on the top of the control ring to crank it up and the minus (–) symbol below to make it quieter.

12. Enjoy.

Meet the iPod

My guess is that you wouldn't be reading these words if an iPod weren't already part of your life—or weren't soon to be part of your life. Congratulations. You've chosen to ally yourself with the world's most popular and—in my humble opinion—finest portable music player.

Oh, sure, there have been pretenders to the throne, countless "iPod killers" that on closer examination proved to be nothing more than less-capable and less-stylish wannabes. Despite multiple attempts to diminish its dominance, the iPod remains It—*the* music player to own.

And now that you do, it's time to become better acquainted with your multimedia buddy. To get started, let's tour the various iPod models and rummage around in the iPod's box.

Today's iPods

The danger of slapping a heading like "Today's iPods" in a book like this one is that—given Apple's habit of revving at least some portion of the iPod line every 9 to 12 months—Today's iPods may be Yesterday's iPods by the time you read this chapter. Unless the next-generation iPods breathe fire and project high-definition movies, however, the iPod you own shouldn't be disturbingly different from what I'm writing about in the autumn of 2009. Here's the lineup.

iPod touch

The iPod touch is so different from the click-wheel iPods and iPod shuffle that rather than force touch owners to skip through this book, cherry-picking the bits that apply to their device, I've devoted an entire book to it: *The iPod touch Pocket Guide* (also from Peachpit Press).

That said, it would be odd to completely exclude an Apple device with the iPod name attached to it. So I'll give it the briefest mention here with the understanding that I'll rarely talk about it again.

In the early summer of 2007, Apple released a little something called the iPhone. Maybe you've heard of it. With the iPhone came the promise of an iPod that could be controlled not by a wheel or series of buttons, but by the touch of a finger. A few months later, the iPod touch delivered on that promise. A year after that, an updated version with a volume switch and an internal speaker appeared. And a year after *that,* Apple released an iPod touch with greater capacity and a faster processor. Like the iPhone, the iPod touch bears a touchscreen display that you control by tapping, flicking, pinching, and dragging objects on its screen.

The iPod touch is sort of a hybrid between a regular iPod and the iPhone. As I mention earlier in this section, it has a display and interface similar to the iPhone's. It also includes wireless networking circuitry (Wi-Fi). It has the same media capabilities as the iPhone, letting you play music and videos, view slideshows, and watch YouTube videos streamed across the Web. And just as you can with an iPhone, you can purchase music and third-party applications directly from the iPod touch via Apple's iTunes Store and App Store, respectively.

iPod classic: Second generation (2G)

To keep the various iPod models straight in the past, I've referred to the many full-size iPod models by their generation. The original iPod was the first-generation (1G) iPod. Apple named five generations of these full-size players simply *iPod* until, with the introduction of the iPod touch in the autumn of 2007, the company added the word *classic* to distinguish the old full-size iPod from the fuller-size iPod touch.

But the hits just keep on coming, and in September 2009, the company issued an iPod classic no different from the previous version except for greater storage capacity (160 GB versus the previous model's 120 GB).

Like Apple, I'll call both of these iPods 2G iPod classics, but where necessary, I'll distinguish each model by its year of release: 2008 and 2009.

Whereas there were two iPod classic models when this iPod was first released—in capacities of 80 GB and 160 GB—today, there's just one. That one is the $249 160 GB iPod classic (**Figure 1.1** on the next page), available in silver or black. It sports a bright 2.5-inch display (measured diagonally) and a colorful interface featuring album artwork in the first couple of layers. It holds up to 40,000 4-minute, 128 Kbps AAC songs (or just over 111 days of continuous music); 200 hours of video encoded with Apple's H.264 video encoder at a resolution of 640 by 480 pixels; or 25,000 photos.

Figure 1.1

iPod classic.

PHOTO COURTESY OF APPLE, INC.

The iPod classic, like all iPods, operates on a rechargeable lithium-ion polymer battery. Apple estimates that constant play time between charges clocks in at around 36 hours for music or around 6 hours for video—if you refrain from mucking too much with the iPod's controls, switch off EQ and Sound Check, and leave backlighting off. (In Chapter 8, I tell you how to get the greatest life out of that battery charge.) In a play-time test, I got 42 hours and 17 minutes of audio and, after fully recharging the thing, nearly 7.5 hours of continuous video on my 2G iPod classic.

note Those who know something of iPod history may recall that the 1G iPod classic came in a 160 GB capacity. The next release reduced that capacity to 120 GB, and with the 2009 iPod classic, the capacity returned to 160 GB. Why? In 2008, the company that makes the classic's hard drive didn't offer a 160 GB model that would fit inside the iPod, so Apple had to offer the lower-capacity drive. In 2009, such a 160 GB drive did exist, enabling Apple to return to the larger-capacity model.

iPod nano: Fifth generation (5G)

The 5G iPod nano (**Figure 1.2**) can be silver, black, purple, blue, green, yellow, orange, pink, or (PRODUCT) RED. A portion of the price of the (PRODUCT) RED nano goes to the Global Fund to Fight AIDS in Africa.

Figure 1.2

iPod nano.

PHOTO COURTESY OF APPLE, INC.

This nano is colorful on the inside as well; just like the iPod classic, it can show pictures and slideshows, colorful album art, and video. Also like the classic, the sleek nano bears a crisp, colorful TFT (thin film transistor) LCD display (2.2 inches measured diagonally, rather than 2.5 inches) and sports a click-wheel control. Like its larger siblings, it has a Dock connector on the bottom and a hold switch on the top; unlike those iPods, it has the headphone port on the bottom.

Unlike any other iPod, it bears an FM radio, video camera, external microphone, and a pedometer that counts your steps. I devote Chapter 3 to the nano's unique talents.

Like the iPod touch, the nano bears something called an *accelerometer*—a motion detector. When you hold the nano upright, you view its content in *portrait* orientation; you can view content in *landscape* orientation by turning the nano on its side. What you see then depends on what screen the iPod is currently displaying. (In Chapter 3, I describe the nano's navigation and orientation features in detail.)

Apple offers the latest model in two configurations: the $149 8 GB iPod nano and the $179 16 GB iPod nano. The 8 GB nano holds approximately 2,000 songs, and the 16 GB version can pack in up to 4,000 songs. The lower-capacity model can hold up to 7,000 pictures, whereas the 16 GB nano can carry up to 14,000 photos.

Unlike the iPod classic and the larger iPods before it, the nano has no internal moving parts. Instead of a hard drive, it uses flash-media chips—solid-state storage circuitry—to store music and data. In addition to being tiny, these chips offer a singular advantage: They make playback skip-proof. Playback on an iPod classic can skip if you're playing long or large tracks or if you bounce around a lot, as you might while exercising. This issue doesn't come up with the nano, as music is fed immediately from the flash chip to the nano's amplifier. This arrangement makes the nano an ideal workout companion. (The iPod shuffle, which is the subject of the next section, also uses flash media.)

But what if you *want* the 5G nano to skip? You can make it shuffle to a different track simply by playing a track and then shaking the nano vigorously. This "shake to shuffle" feature is unique to the 4G and 5G iPod nanos, iPod shuffles, and iPhones.

Battery life on the nano is respectable. Apple claims approximately 24 hours of music play time, but I've managed to make my 8 GB nano play music for nearly 30 hours. Apple's suggestion that the nano will play video for around 5 hours is accurate.

iPod shuffle: Third generation (3G)

The iPod shuffle is famous for being the "displayless" iPod. Starting with
the 3G model (**Figure 1.3**), it's also the only "buttonless" iPod. Unlike the
previous shuffle models, which include buttons for controlling the device,
this iPod lets you play and navigate its music library via a small controller incorporated into the headset cord. With that controller, you can
pause and play your music, adjust volume, and skip to another playlist.
Optionally, using Apple's VoiceOver technology, the 3G iPod shuffle can
speak the name of the currently playing song and its performing artist.
It can also speak the names of the playlists stored on the iPod, making it
possible to navigate playlists by using audio cues only.

Figure 1.3
iPod shuffle.

PHOTO COURTESY OF APPLE, INC.

Unlike the other iPods, the shuffle has no Dock-connector port. Instead, it
sports a headphone port that also acts as a data syncing and power port.
To sync and charge the shuffle, string the included USB cable between
the iPod's headphone port and your computer's USB 2.0 port.

The 3G iPod shuffle can be had in 2 GB ($59) and 4 GB ($79) configurations, holding approximately 500 and 1,000 songs, respectively. It's available in silver, black, blue, green, and pink. Apple has also created a special-edition 3G iPod shuffle with a polished silver stainless-steel case. This shuffle costs $99 and has 4 GB of storage. As I mention earlier in this chapter, the shuffle uses flash memory rather than a hard drive, which makes it another good choice for the gym.

This iPod also has a rechargeable lithium-ion polymer battery (a very, very small one). Apple rates the shuffle's constant play time between charges at around 10 hours. I've managed just over 12 hours of constant use from mine.

Given the shuffle's price and size, you can understand that it has certain limitations. The lack of a display is the most obvious one. This iPod is not the one to own if you want to find and play a specific track easily. Instead, you should think of the shuffle as your personal radio station—one that you've programmed with your favorite music so that you won't care which song it plays.

Because it lacks a display, the shuffle doesn't hold pictures, contacts, or calendars, which other iPod models can display. It can't record audio from an outside source, either. The shuffle is exactly what it appears to be: a basic music player.

Thinking Inside the Box

At one time, Apple stuffed the iPod box with loads of goodies: in-ear headphones, a couple of cables for transferring data between your computer and iPod, a power adapter, a Dock and case for more-expensive iPods, a belt clip (for the iPod mini), a video cable for iPods with color screens, a software CD, documentation, and (of course) the iPod itself. Rummage around in the box of an iPod you've purchased in the past couple of months, and you'll find that many of these items are missing, available now only as $29 to $49 add-ons.

No worries—what *is* in the box provides you enough to get started. Here's what you'll find inside the various iPod boxes.

Earbuds

Your iPod comes with a set of headphones that you place inside—rather than over—your ears. Headphones of this style are known as *earbuds*. A pair of foam earbud covers accompanied earlier iPods; Apple now offers an earbud design that lacks these disks.

Just as you'll find a wide range of foot and head sizes among groups of people, the sizes of ear openings vary. The earbuds included with 1G iPods were a little larger than other earbuds you may have seen. Some people (including your humble author) found them uncomfortable. Later iPods included smaller earbuds that many people found much more comfortable. I find that without the foam covers, the latest headphones don't fit my ears terribly well; they just won't stay in a position where I can hear the audio sweet spot. If, like me, you find the earbuds unsatisfactory, you can purchase smaller or larger earbuds, or you can opt for a pair of over-the-ear headphones.

If the included earbuds *do* fit you, you may or may not be pleased with their performance. Apple made great efforts to create the finest music player on the planet and didn't skimp on the headphones, but sound is subjective, and you may find that other headphones deliver a more pleasing sound to your ears. If you believe that you deserve better sound than your Apple earbuds provide, by all means audition other headphones.

USB 2.0 cable

The iPod's proprietary Dock connector (that thin port on the bottom of all iPods save the shuffle) is the avenue for transferring both music and information on and off the iPod and for charging the device. Likewise, the USB 2.0 cable included with the iPod can perform double duty. When you string the cable between your iPod and your computer's powered USB 2.0 port, power flows through the cable and charges the iPod's battery. At the same time, this connection allows you to swap data—in the form of music and other files—between the player and the computer.

 The USB cable can also be attached to the optional $29 Apple USB Power Adapter to charge the iPod's battery when the iPod isn't connected to a computer.

iPod Dock Adapter (click-wheel iPods only)

This adapter looks similar to the cradle adapters included with some iPod accessories. To assist iPod accessory manufacturers, which were forced to come up with a new cradle design every time Apple issued a new iPod, Apple created a single one-size-fits-all-with-the-right-Apple-adapter specification for companies that participate in the Made for iPod program. This is that adapter. Currently, many accessories—including speakers and Docks—support this universal adapter.

Guides and documentation

It seems that you can't buy something as simple as a toaster these days without gaining mounds of accompanying documentation. Apple is different in this regard. The current iPods come with a slim Quick Start guide and a product-information pamphlet that carries the fine print.

Given that you own this book, you can skip nearly all the paperwork that comes with your iPod (unless reading the fine print of licensing agreements helps you sleep at night). At one time, I would have sent you to the bundled CD to gawk at Apple's iPod manual or to install iTunes, but Apple has dispensed with the CD, figuring that you can obtain iTunes and any technical information from its Web site.

Yesterday's iPods

I'd like to think that a lot of old iPods are being passed from person to person as the original owners trade up. It's quite possible that you have an older iPod yet are new to this whole iPod business. This section is for you. Here's how the various models shake out.

iPod: First generation (1G)

As the name implies, these models are the very first iPods, released in late 2001 and early 2002. The 1G iPod is offered in 5 GB and 10 GB configurations, and it bears a mechanical scroll wheel—a wheel that actually turns, unlike the one on later iPods. Nothing on the back of an original 5 GB iPod indicates its storage capacity; the 10 GB model is marked as such on the back plate. These iPods support FireWire connections only and are incompatible with today's Dock-connector accessories. They also don't play files in Apple Lossless format or record audio from an external source. Like all iPods up to the current full-size iPod, this iPod is incapable of playing video files.

iPod: Second generation (2G)

The second white iPod comes in 5, 10, and 20 GB capacities; sports a touch-sensitive scroll wheel; includes redesigned earbuds that fit smaller ear canals more comfortably; and slaps a plastic cover over the FireWire port. This iPod has the same limitations as the 1G iPod in terms of support for Apple Lossless, Dock-connector accessories, audio recording, and video playback.

iPod: Third generation (3G)

Whereas the 2G iPods were an evolutionary release, the 3G players are a redefinition of the original. These iPods—available in capacities of 10, 15, 20, 30, and 40 GB—are sleeker and lighter. They feature an updated front-panel design that places touch-sensitive (and backlit) navigation buttons above the scroll wheel. Gone is the FireWire connector at the top of the iPod, replaced by a proprietary connector at the bottom of the unit that supports both FireWire and USB 2.0 connections. (Charging over USB is not supported on these iPods, however.) An updated remote connector is also added to the top of the 3G iPod. This connector is ostensibly for connecting the Apple iPod Remote to the player, but it's also used by other accessories, such as Griffin Technology's iTrip FM transmitter and Belkin's Voice Recorder for iPod.

iPod mini: First and second generations (1G and 2G)

In January 2004, Apple released a smaller version of the iPod: the iPod mini. The 1G mini is available in five colors: gold, silver, blue, green, and pink. The original mini is the first iPod to hold a 4 GB hard drive (called a *microdrive*), as well as the first iPod to sport a click wheel. The 2G mini comes in brighter shades of blue, green, and pink (gold was discontinued after 1G, and the silver model looks the same as the 1G version) and in 4 GB and 6 GB configurations. The mini was discontinued with the introduction of the iPod nano.

iPod: Fourth generation (4G)

When Apple announced the 4G iPod in July 2004, it could have done so by proclaiming that the "maxi-mini" was born, for in some ways, the 4G iPod is closer in design to the iPod mini than to the previous three generations of white iPods. Available in 20 GB and 40 GB configurations, the 4G iPod bears the same kind of click-wheel controller used on the mini, and like the mini, it can be charged via USB 2.0.

Apple iPod + HP, Apple iPod mini + HP, Apple iPod shuffle + HP

At one time, Hewlett-Packard sold iPods. No longer. These iPods are unique because . . . well, because they were sold by HP. They're identical to Apple's iPods with the exception of the warranty: HP's warranty was a bit more generous in terms of when you'd have to begin paying to have your iPod fixed. HP canceled its iPod partnership with Apple in the summer of 2005.

iPod U2 Special Edition (monochrome version)

Though functionally identical to a 20 GB monochrome 4G iPod, this special player is the first "big" iPod to come in colors—specifically, a black face with a red click wheel. This special iPod also carries the signatures of the four U2 members etched on the back plate.

iPod photo

You can think of the iPod photo as being either a 4G iPod with color and photo capabilities or as the succeeding color-display iPod with *photo* appended to its name. This iPod—available in capacities of 30, 40, and 60 GB—is the higher-priced alternative to the monochrome 4G iPod. In addition to putting a bright and colorful face on the now-dull-in-comparison 4G iPod, the iPod photo allows you to view pictures and slideshows on your iPod (up to 25,000 pictures on the 60 GB model), as well as to project those pictures on an attached television set or compatible projector.

iPod with color display

Apple did little more than make this iPod's name more cumbersome to differentiate it from the earlier iPod photo; it sports no change worthy of terming it the 5G iPod. Beginning with this model, all full-size iPods offer color. The iPod with color display comes in 20, 30, and 60 GB configurations.

iPod shuffle: First generation (1G)

The original iPod shuffle is about the size of a pack of gum and can be had in capacities of 512 MB and 1 GB. Unlike the current shuffle, this one bears a male USB connector, which allows you to jack the iPod into your computer's USB port without the need for a Dock.

iPod nano: First generation (1G)

This model is the original iPod nano. Its face is easily scratched plastic, and its back is shiny silver, like the backs of full-size iPods. It comes in capacities of 1, 2, and 4 GB and in just two colors (black and white), and it doesn't support voice memos.

iPod: Fifth generation (5G)

This iPod is the original iPod with video. It differs from the late-2006 model in that its screen isn't as bright, and it doesn't offer that model's alphabetic search feature (more on this in Chapter 4).

iPod: Fifth generation (5G), late 2006

Some wags refer to this model as the 5.5G iPod. As I just stated, it has a brighter screen than the original 5G iPod, as well as a search feature that's missing from the original 5G.

iPod nano: Second generation (2G)

The 2G nano has the same longish body as the original nano, but it sports a full metal jacket reminiscent of the iPod mini. It comes in silver, blue, green, pink, (PRODUCT) RED, and black, and in capacities of 2, 4, and 8 GB. Unlike the somewhat squattier 3G nano, it has a 1.5-inch color screen and doesn't play video.

iPod shuffle: Second generation (2G)

Apple made the shuffle even smaller with this design. About the size of a large postage stamp, though much thicker, the 2G shuffle features a large Play button (well, large given the size of the iPod) surrounded by a ring for controlling such functions as volume, next, previous, fast-forward, and rewind. It includes a special Dock for syncing the iPod with iTunes. Over the years, Apple has offered this shuffle in a variety of colors.

iPod classic: First generation (1G)

As I state earlier in the chapter, Apple gave the full-size iPod a new name—iPod classic—when it introduced the iPod nano in the autumn of 2007. The 1G classic is offered in black and silver brushed-aluminum cases with capacities of 80 GB and 160 GB.

iPod nano: Third generation (3G)

With the third version of the iPod nano, Apple expanded the screen to 2 inches (measured diagonally) and made the body squattier. This "wide-load" nano comes in five colors—silver, green, blue, black, and (PRODUCT) RED—and in two capacities—4 GB and 8 GB. With the 3G nano, Apple brought feature parity to the nano and full-size iPod lines. Before this model, the classic had features that the nano didn't, such as video playback.

iPod nano: Fourth generation (4G)

The 4G nano, released in September 2008, returns to the longer case design used in the first two generations of nanos. It isn't simply a redo of these models, however. The 4G iPod nano introduces a longer screen (2 inches measured diagonally). It also offers better storage, Genius playlist support, the Spoken Menus feature, and the accelerometer.

Phoning It In

When is an iPod not an iPod—and, therefore, worthy of nothing more than this small sidebar? When it's a phone (and no, I don't mean *that* phone). Motorola was the first company to release an iTunes-compatible mobile phone: the ill-fated ROKR. Why ill-fated? It was a little clunky-looking; it took forever to sync music because of its USB 1.1 interface; and it held a scant 100 tracks. Motorola later released the SLVR, a sleeker phone, but it suffers the same 100-track limit and slow USB 1.1 data-transfer rate.

2

Controls and Interface

The iPod has rightly been praised for its ease of use. As with all its products, Apple strove to make the iPod as intuitive as possible, placing a limited number of controls and ports on the device and making moving from one screen to another a logical progression. In the following pages, I scrutinize each iPod's controls and examine the screens that populate the display-bearing iPods.

On the Face of It

On the front of an iPod classic or iPod nano, you'll find a display and set of navigation controls. The shuffle has no display; its controls are located on the headset. On the first two generations (1G and 2G) of the iPod, these controls are arrayed around a central click wheel and are mechanical—meaning that they move and activate switches underneath the buttons. On the 3G iPods, these controls are placed above the click wheel and are touch-sensitive; they activate when they come into contact with your flesh but, allegedly, not when a nonfleshy object (such as the walls of your backpack, pocket, or purse) touches them.

The iPod mini, the 4G and later full-size iPods, and the iPod nano bear a click wheel that incorporates the navigation buttons. Unlike the first two generations of the iPod, on which the buttons are arrayed around the outside of the wheel, these iPods feature buttons that are part of the wheel itself (**Figure 2.1**). The buttons' sensors sit beneath the wheel at the four compass points, and the click wheel sits on a short spindle that allows it to rock in all directions. To activate one of the buttons, just press the wheel in the direction of that button.

Figure 2.1
iPod's click wheel.

The 3G iPod shuffle's navigation controls are based on three buttons on the control incorporated into the cord of the right earbud. The top button increases volume, and the bottom button turns it down. The Center button has a variety of functions, including play/pause, next, previous, fast-forward, rewind, and playlist selection. Because the shuffle lacks a display and has unique controls, I discuss it separately in this chapter.

The iPod display

Near the top of an iPod classic sits a 2.5-inch-diagonal, color liquid crystal display that can show up to 65,536 colors at a resolution of 320 by 240 pixels. Like the nano's, the classic iPod's display features backlighting (illumination that makes the display easier to read in dim light), which you can switch on simply by touching the click wheel. (On older iPods, you switch on backlighting by pressing the Menu button.) By default, the backlight is configured to shine for 10 seconds.

Measured diagonally, the color display of the 5G nano is 0.3 inch smaller than that of the iPod classic, yet it projects more text than its sibling because it's taller. The taller screen isn't the only factor, however. The iPod nano also uses a different font from the one used on the iPod classic and also has greater pixel density (meaning that it packs in more pixels per inch onscreen).

iPod classic and iPod nano controls

The controls of the iPod classics and iPod nanos are identical, so it makes sense to discuss them together.

Play/Pause button

If you scan the surface of your iPod classic or iPod nano, you'll notice that it bears no recognizable on/off switch. To switch on a current iPod classic or iPod nano, press the Center button. This same technique works with the 5G iPod; the original iPod classic; and the 1G, 2G, 3G, and 4G iPod nanos.

On models earlier than the 5G iPod, start up by using the Play/Pause button. To switch off any display-bearing iPod, press and hold its

Play/Pause button for about 3 seconds. This button is located at the bottom of the iPod control wheel on older iPods, in the third position in the row of buttons on 3G iPods, and at the bottom of the click wheel on today's iPod classics and iPod nano. As you'd expect, pressing this button also starts and pauses music, video playback, and photo slideshows. On a 5G iPod nano, it pauses and plays FM radio too.

Each of these iPods includes a preview area—a place where you can see album or video art or learn how much free space remains on your iPod. On the classic, the preview area is on the right side of the display; on the nano, it's at the bottom.

Previous button

This button is located on the far-left side of the wheel on 1G, 2G, and click-wheel iPods; it's the far-left button on 3G iPods. In most cases, pressing this button once takes you to the beginning of the currently playing song or video.

note   Click-wheel iPods are capable of playing a variety of videos: TV shows, movies, music videos, video podcasts, and (in the case of the 5G iPod nano) videos you've captured with the built-in camera. When I mention video in a generic sense, I'm speaking of all these different kinds of videos.

The exception involves movies that you purchased or rented from the iTunes Store, audiobooks, and enhanced podcasts. If these items have chapter marks (and all do, as far as I know), pressing Previous moves the movie, audiobook, or podcast to the previous chapter. Press Previous multiple times to move back multiple chapters. If, with a movie, you've pressed Previous more times than the movie has chapters, you're taken back to the Movies screen.

When you press Previous twice while listening to an audiobook's first chapter, you'll be taken to the previous section of that audiobook (Part 1 if you were listening to Part 2, for example) or, if there is no previous section, to the audiobook whose entry in the Audiobooks screen appears above the one you're listening to. If you're already listening to the first entry in this list, you're taken to the Audiobooks screen.

Similarly, for an enhanced podcast, if you press Previous, and some episodes of this particular podcast appear above the one you're currently listening to in that podcast's list of episodes, you'll be taken to the beginning of the previous episode. Suppose that you have episodes of NPR's *Fresh Air* on your iPod, and you're listening to the third episode in the list. Pressing Previous at the beginning of that third episode will cause the iPod to play the second episode from the beginning. Press Previous again, and you hear the first episode in the list. Press Previous one more time, and you're taken back to that podcast's list of episodes.

Pressing Previous twice in succession in a music playlist moves you to the previous song in the playlist. Do this with a video track, and you're taken back to the Video screen or to that video's playlist screen. Hold down Previous to rewind through a song, video, movie, audiobook, or podcast. When you rewind or fast-forward through a song, video, audiobook, or podcast, you move in small increments at first; as you continue to hold the button down, you move in larger increments.

On iPods with a color display, the Previous button also moves you back through a slideshow.

Next button

Look to the far right on 1G, 2G, and click-wheel iPods; look to the rightmost button on 3G iPods. This button behaves similarly to the Previous button. Press it when you're viewing a movie or listening to a chaptered audiobook or enhanced podcast to move forward through chapters. Press this button once to go to the next song in a music playlist. Press it once while you're viewing a nonmovie video, and you return to the Video screen or to that video's playlist screen. Hold Next down to fast-forward through a song, video, movie, or podcast. As is true of rewinding, fast-forwarding moves you through small increments of a song, video, audio-book, or podcast at first; as you continue to hold the button down, the increments get larger.

On iPods with a color display, the Next button also advances you through a slideshow.

Menu button

Pressing the well-marked Menu button takes you back through the interface the way you came. If you've moved from the main iPod screen to the Music screen, for example, and you press the Menu button, you'll move back to the main iPod screen. If you've moved from the main iPod screen through the Music screen to the Playlists screen to a particular song within a particular playlist, each time you press the Menu button, you'll move back one screen.

On iPods earlier than the iPod classics and 3G iPod nano, holding the Menu button down for about 2 seconds turns backlighting on or off. On today's iPods, press and hold the Menu button, and you're taken to the iPod's main screen, thereby avoiding what may be a tedious trip back up the hierarchy.

Click wheel

Inside the ring of buttons on 1G and 2G iPods, below the bevy of buttons on 3G iPods, and marked with the navigation controls on Dock-connector iPods is the click wheel. Moving your thumb clockwise highlights items below the selected item; moving your thumb counterclockwise highlights items above the selected item. If a window is larger than the display, moving the click wheel causes the window to scroll up or down when the first or last item in the list is highlighted.

You use the click wheel to adjust volume and to move to a particular location in a song, video, audiobook, or podcast. On a 5G iPod nano, you use the click wheel's scrolling capabilities to select radio stations and pick points in a buffered radio recording to begin playback. (I discuss all things FM radio in Chapter 3.)

Center button

The bull's-eye of all iPods—the Center button—selects a menu item. If the Settings menu item is selected, for example, pressing the Center button moves you to the Settings screen, where you can select additional settings.

When you press the Center button while a song is playing and the Play screen is visible, you move to another Play screen, where you can *scrub* (quickly navigate forward and back with the click wheel) your song or video. On the 2G iPod classic and 5G nano, press this button again, and you can engage the Genius playlist feature (see the next section, "The Genius of click-wheel iPods"). One more press on these iPods, and you move to the Ratings screen, where you can assign a rating of one to five stars to the song by using the click wheel. Press the Center button yet again, and the Shuffle screen appears, where you can tell the iPod to shuffle playback by songs or albums (or not at all, if another shuffle setting has been selected). If you've added lyrics to the song in iTunes (more on this topic in Chapter 4), one more press of the Center button displays those lyrics in the next screen.

While you're watching a movie with chapter marks, pressing the Center button once displays a progress bar that includes the movie's chapter marks. Press the button again, and the scrub control appears. Press one more time, and a brightness bar appears. Just thumb the click wheel up or down to adjust brightness.

If you're listening to a podcast, one press of the Center button reveals the scrub bar, another press shows ratings, and one more press displays a screen where you see information about that podcast episode (the creator's name and a blurb about the episode's content).

For audiobooks, the first press shows the scrub bar; a second press gives you ratings; and a third press takes you back to the first screen, which holds a progress bar and time readouts that detail the audiobook's elapsed and remaining times.

The Genius of click-wheel iPods

With iTunes 8, Apple introduced the compelling Genius feature. I explain Genius as it relates to iTunes in greater detail in Chapter 4, but the gist is this: When you turn on Genius, you voluntarily (and anonymously) submit the contents of your iTunes Library to Apple. In exchange, Apple analyzes that content and sends a database file of related music in your library back to your computer. Using this file, Genius can create playlists of music that it believes will work well with a track that you've selected.

Say that you select The Rolling Stones' "19th Nervous Breakdown" as the source track in iTunes and then click the Genius icon at the bottom of the iTunes window. Genius creates a playlist of 25 tracks that includes classic rock tracks from your iTunes Library—Donovan's "Mellow Yellow," The Allman Brothers' "Whipping Post," and Deep Purple's "Hush," for example.

You can initiate a Genius playlist from the Music screen. The process works like this:

1. Start playing a track, and press the Center button until you see a screen that features the word *Genius* at the bottom.

2. In that screen, scroll the click wheel clockwise so that the arrow at the bottom of the screen moves to the right and you see the blue Genius icon.

In a second or so, the iPod will take you to a Genius screen that lists the song you were playing and 24 additional songs that your iPod believes work well with the original song (**Figure 2.2**).

Figure 2.2

The Genius playlist on a 5G iPod nano.

To refresh this playlist, just select Refresh and then press the Center button. The iPod will cobble together 24 other related tracks.

3. If you like what the iPod came up with, select Save Playlist and then press the Center button.

You move to the Playlists screen, where a new Genius playlist appears, bearing the name of the original track. Select this playlist and press the Center button to see the contents of the playlist; refresh those contents by selecting Refresh and pressing the Center button.

Here's another way to do the same thing: Simply select a song (within a playlist or in an Album, Artist, or Genre screen, for example) and then press and hold the Center button. Do this on a 2G iPod classic, and you're taken to a screen that includes these commands: Start Genius, Add to On-The-Go, Browse Album, Browse Artist, and Cancel. Here, I'll focus on Start Genius. Select it and press the Center button, and the iPod creates a Genius playlist. This playlist works just like the one I describe earlier in this section, and you can refresh or save it.

The 4G and 5G iPod nanos work almost exactly the same way. The difference is that when you press and hold the Center button with a track selected, a small sheet drops down from the top of the screen. This sheet bears the same commands I just mentioned. Select Start Genius, and you've created a Genius playlist based on the selected track.

What if you want to revisit an unsaved Genius playlist on either iPod? Just navigate to the Music screen, select Genius, and press the Center button. You'll be taken to that playlist.

note This press-and-hold-to-create-a-Genius-playlist business doesn't work in Cover Flow view on either iPod model.

iPod shuffle status light and controls

There's no need to mention the shuffle's display, because it has none. It does have a status light that tells you what it's doing, however. The 2G model has controls, whereas the 3G shuffle is controlled via the headphone switch. Both of the clip-on models (meaning the 2G and 3G shuffles) also have power and play-order switches, and the 1G shuffle has a single power/play-order switch on the back. Here's how they work.

The three-position switch (3G iPod shuffle)

The top of the 3G shuffle has a single three-position switch: Off, Play in Order, and Shuffle (**Figure 2.3**). Push the power switch one notch to turn the shuffle on and enter Play in Order mode, which plays the currently selected playlist from beginning to end and then cycles back to the beginning of the playlist. Push the switch as far from the Off position as possible, and you enter Shuffle mode. In Shuffle mode, the iPod plays songs within the current playlist in random order. (No, the iPod doesn't shuffle among playlists.)

Figure 2.3
3G iPod shuffle's three-position switch, LED, and headphone port.

When you move the switch to Play in Order mode, you'll hear three ascending tones (a major triad, for you musicians out there). Choose Shuffle mode, and you hear four descending tones.

> **tip** If you're listening to an audiobook or want to listen to podcast episodes in the order in which they were produced, choose Play in Order rather than Shuffle. Fail to do so, and the audiobook's chapters and podcast episodes will be presented in random order.

Power and play-order switches (2G iPod shuffle)

The top of the 2G shuffle has two switches: one for power and another that toggles between Play in Order and Shuffle modes (**Figure 2.4**). Push the power switch to the right to turn the shuffle on. Push the play-order switch to the left, and the iPod lives up to its name and shuffles its playlist randomly. Push this switch to the right, and the shuffle plays its playlist, in order, from beginning to end before repeating.

Figure 2.4
2G iPod shuffle's power and play-order switches.

note Because this shuffle and the original iPod shuffle can hold only a single playlist, you can imagine that mixing audiobook chapters with other tracks and then switching on Shuffle mode would make for a unique listening experience. To help prevent this sort of thing, Apple won't let you copy audiobooks and podcasts automatically to a 1G or 2G shuffle. Instead, you must copy them manually (indicating that you really want them on the iPod). I talk much more about syncing in Chapter 4.

Status light

The top and bottom of the clip-on iPod shuffles feature small light-emitting diodes (LEDs). When you first turn on a fully charged shuffle, a light on these LEDs glows green for about 3 seconds. If the shuffle has a low charge, you'll see an amber light for those 3 seconds. A really low charge produces a red light. You get no glow at all when there's no charge.

When you press Play (or any part of the outer ring) on a 2G shuffle or press the Center button on a 3G shuffle's headset controller, the green light briefly appears again. If you pause playback on a 2G iPod shuffle, the green light blinks for a minute. Do the same on a 3G shuffle, and the light blinks for 30 seconds. In general, other commands—Volume Up and Down, Next Track, Previous Track, Fast Forward, Rewind, Hear Playlist Menu (3G shuffle), and Exit Playlist Menu (3G shuffle)—produce a green blink. (Those blinks are longer for Play, Rewind, and Fast Forward on a 2G iPod shuffle.)

When you plug the shuffle into a power source, the amber LED light glows continuously until the shuffle is fully charged; then the light switches to green.

Headset controls (3G iPod shuffle only)

As I mention earlier in this chapter, the 3G iPod shuffle is controlled entirely by the headset controller embedded in the right earbud's cord (**Figure 2.5**).

Figure 2.5

The 3G iPod shuffle's headset controller.

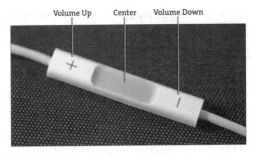

Volume Up   Center   Volume Down

The controller has three buttons, which you use this way:

■ **Play or pause.** Press the Center button to toggle between Play and Pause.

■ **Adjust the volume.** Press the Volume Up button (at the top of the controller) to increment the volume one notch. Press the Volume Down button (at the bottom of the controller) to turn the volume down one notch.

■ **Skip to the next track.** Double-press the Center button.

■ **Move to the previous track.** Triple-press the Center button when the track has been playing for fewer than 6 seconds. If the track has been playing for longer than 6 seconds, triple-press to move to the beginning of the playing track and then triple-press again to move to the previous track.

■ **Fast-forward the current track.** Double-press and hold the Center button.

■ **Rewind the current track.** Triple-press and hold the Center button.

■ **Hear the track title and artist name.** Press and hold the Center button.

■ **Choose a playlist.** Press and hold the Center button until you hear a tone. The iPod begins reciting the names of playlists on the iPod. When you hear the playlist you want to listen to, press the Center button again.

tip If you have a lot of playlists on your iPod shuffle and want to dash through them, press the Volume Up or Volume Down button. With each press, you move to the next (Volume Up) or previous (Volume Down) playlist.

Outer ring (2G iPod shuffle only)

The ring that surrounds the inner Play/Pause button on the 2G iPod shuffle (**Figure 2.6**) handles track "navigation" (such as it is) and volume control. Press the top of the ring (marked with +) to increase volume; press the bottom of the ring (marked with –) to turn the volume down. The right side of the ring controls the iPod's Next function; press once to move to the next track, or press and hold to fast-forward through the current track.

Figure 2.6

2G iPod shuffle's outer ring.

The Previous button on the left side of the ring works like the Previous buttons on other iPods. Press once, and the currently playing song starts again at the beginning. Press twice quickly in succession to move to the previous song in the playlist.

Play/Pause button (2G iPod shuffle only)

Yes, the Play/Pause button does what it says. With the 2G shuffle switched on, press the button once to play; press it again to pause.

Because the shuffle has so few controls, Apple has pressed this button into service to perform other jobs. To go to the beginning of a playlist, for example, press Play/Pause three times quickly (within a second). To lock the iPod (disable its buttons), press and hold the button for about 3 seconds. To unlock it, press and hold the button again.

note **When you lock the shuffle, its status light blinks three times. When you unlock it, the light briefly glows green.**

Battery-status button/light

Unlike the original iPod shuffle, which carries its own battery status light, the clip-on iPod shuffles indicate their current charge through the LED on the top. To see how much charge you have left, quickly flick the power switch off and then on. The shuffle will continue playing if you do this rapidly enough. A green-glowing LED indicates a full charge (even after the shuffle has played for several hours). If you see an amber light, the shuffle is low on power. A red light indicates that it's *really* low on power, and no light at all tells you that the shuffle is completely drained and should be plugged into a power source to charge.

Ports and connectors: Dock-connector iPods

The iPod doesn't work by osmosis. You need a hole for the sound to get out (and, in some cases, in) and another hole for moving data on and off the device. Here's what you'll find on today's iPods.

Headphone port and hold switch

The 3G and all click-wheel iPods except the iPod nano, 5G iPod, and iPod classics sport a headphone port, a hold switch, and an iPod Remote Control connector up top (**Figure 2.7** and **Figure 2.8**).

Figure 2.7
Top of the 4G iPod.

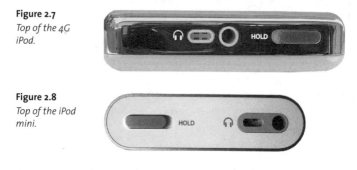

Figure 2.8
Top of the iPod mini.

You'll find the 3G iPod nano's hold switch and headphone port on the bottom (**Figure 2.9**). The 4G and 5G iPod nanos' headphone port is also on the bottom, but the hold switch is on top (**Figure 2.10**).

Figure 2.9
Bottom of the 3G iPod nano.

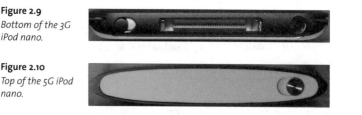

Figure 2.10
Top of the 5G iPod nano.

Today's iPods have no Remote Control port. The headphone port and hold switch provide audio output and disable the iPod's controls, respectively, working nearly the same way on today's iPods and iPod nanos as they do on older models.

tip I say *nearly* because the headphone port, in combination with the Remote Control connector on 3G-and-later standard iPods up to the 5G iPod, supports not only audio output, but also audio input. With a compatible microphone, you can record low-quality audio (8 kHz) on these iPods. Display-bearing iPods—including the 5G iPod, 2G and 3G iPod nanos, and original iPod classic—support higher-resolution audio recording via their Dock-connector ports and a compatible microphone. The 4G and 5G iPod nanos and the 2G iPod classic support audio recording via the headphone port.

note The 5G iPod can also transmit composite video via its headphone port with a compatible cable. The iPod classics and the 3G, 4G, and 5G iPod nanos can transmit composite or component video from their Dock-connector ports with a compatible accessory or cable.

Dock-connector port

On the bottom of a Dock-connector iPod, you'll find a proprietary port that handles both power and data chores for the device. This port, on the bottom of the 3G iPods and all click-wheel iPods save the iPod nano and the 5G iPod, supports data transfer via both FireWire and USB 2.0 (**Figure 2.11**). The first three generations of nanos, the 5G iPod, and both the 1G and 2G iPod classics can be charged via FireWire and USB but sync only over USB. The 4G and 5G iPod nanos can be charged only with a USB connection.

Figure 2.11
Bottom of the iPod classic.

Ports and connectors: iPod shuffle

The iPod shuffle has exactly one hole: the headphone port. On the original iPod shuffle, this port is exactly what its name implies: a place to plug in your earbuds or other headphones.

The clip-on iPod shuffles' headphone port (refer to Figure 2.3 earlier in this chapter) allows you to do two things: listen to music through it, and sync and charge the iPod through it via the shuffle's Dock. To charge or sync your 3G shuffle, plug the cylindrical end of the USB cable into the headphone port and the USB end into a powered USB 2.0 port on your computer.

To charge or sync a 2G shuffle, plug the Dock cable into a powered USB 2.0 port on your computer; then slip the shuffle into the Dock so that its headphone port slides over the Dock's miniplug.

The original shuffle charges and syncs differently. Flip this shuffle over, pull off its protective cap, and spy the USB connector. Plug that connector into your computer's powered USB 2.0 port to charge the iPod and then transfer music and data to it.

Navigating the Screens

Considering how easy the iPod is to use, it's hard to believe the number of navigation screens that make up its interface. In the following pages, I scrutinize each screen. At one time, the iPod classic and iPod nano had exactly the same interface, but the 4G nano brought to the midsize iPod a couple of talents that are missing from the more capacious classic (and the 5G brought even more compelling talents). I'll be sure to point out how those talents are reflected in the nano's interface.

Main screen

The main screen (**Figure 2.12**), which displays the word *iPod* at the top, is your gateway to the iPod. In a way, it's akin to the Mac's Finder or Windows' My Computer window—a place to get started.

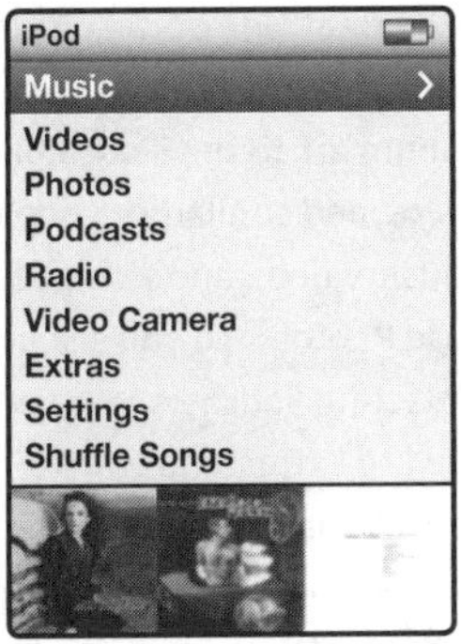

Figure 2.12

5G iPod nano's main screen.

You'll find these commands on today's iPod classic and iPod nano:

- Music

- Videos

- Photos

- Podcasts

- Radio (5G iPod nano only)

- Video Camera (5G iPod nano only)

- Extras

- Voice Memos (if you've plugged in a compatible microphone or recorded and saved any voice memos)

- Settings

- Shuffle Songs

- Now Playing (if a song is playing or paused)

The iPod classics and the 3G–5G iPod nanos offer a split-screen view. (Previous iPods list commands only.) On the classics and the 3G nano, these commands are arrayed along the left side of the display, and different graphics appear on the right side of the display; the kind of graphic you see depends on which command you've selected. If Music is selected, and you've synced album art to the iPod, album covers swoop across the display. Choose Videos, and similarly swooping still images from the movies, TV shows, music videos, and video podcasts on your iPod appear in this area. Choose Photos, and you see previews of the photos stored on your iPod. Selecting Podcasts tells you how many podcasts are on your iPod. Scroll to Extras, and you see the time and date. Select Settings, and you'll see how many gigabytes of free space the iPod has (or megabytes, if you have less than 1 GB of storage free). Choose Shuffle Songs, and the iPod tells you the number of songs stored on it. Finally, scroll to Now Playing, and you see the name, artist, and album of the currently playing track.

The 4G and 5G nanos' information display is a bit different: Artwork is shown at the bottom of the screen. On the 4G nano, the artwork and information that appear here are the same as on the 2G iPod classic, save that choosing Extras displays the artwork for the three Apple games bundled with the nano. The 5G nano additionally includes the Radio entry, which, when selected, displays the station the iPod is tuned to (107.5, for example).

note If, in iTunes, you've chosen to not sync artwork to your iPod, selecting Music or Videos displays a gray screen on the right side (3G nano and iPod classics) or bottom (4G and 5G iPod nanos) of the display that details the number of songs or videos, respectively, on these iPods.

Here's what you'll find within each area.

Music

When you choose the Music command and press the Center button, the resulting Music screen reveals these entries on the 2G iPod classic:

Cover Flow, Genius, Playlists, Artists, Albums, Compilations, Songs, Genres, Composers, Audiobooks, and Search (**Figure 2.13**). I explain the purposes of all these entries in the following sections. On the 4G and 5G iPod nanos, the Compilations entry is missing. On a 5G iPod nano, Genius Mixes— a feature in iTunes 9 that creates nine genre-based albums pulled from your iTunes Library—replaces Genius. (I discuss Genius Mixes in greater depth later in this chapter and in Chapter 4.)

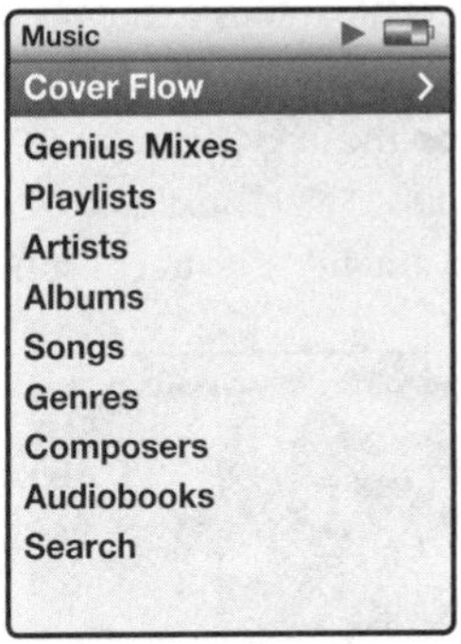

Figure 2.13
5G iPod nano's Music screen.

Music	▶ ▭
Cover Flow	**›**
Genius Mixes	
Playlists	
Artists	
Albums	
Songs	
Genres	
Composers	
Audiobooks	
Search	

Cover Flow (3G–5G iPod nanos and iPod classics only)

Both iPod classics and the 3G–5G iPod nanos include a Cover Flow view—a way to view your music collection by album cover. Select Cover Flow and press the Center button, and you'll see your iPod's music collection as a series of album covers, sorted by the artists' names. Swirl your finger around the click wheel to move through the album covers. When you find an album you like, press the Center button; the cover flips around to reveal the tracks it contains.

Use the usual scrolling gesture to move down the list of tracks and select the one you want; then press the Center button to play it. When you do, the track appears in the iPod's Now Playing screen, where you can adjust its volume and perform the tricks you can do in any other Now Playing screen. The one difference is that when you press the Menu button, you return to Cover Flow view rather than go back to an album screen or menu. To leave Cover Flow view, just press Menu; you'll return to the Music screen.

With 4G and 5G nanos, you can initiate Cover Flow in an additional way. When you're viewing the main screen or the Music screen, or when you're in an area within the Music screen (Albums or Genres, for example), just turn the nano sideways. Cover Flow view appears, showing you the album covers of all the songs stored on the iPod (**Figure 2.14**). You navigate and play songs just as I describe above. Select an album cover and press the Center button to flip the cover around to its track list (**Figure 2.15**).

Figure 2.14

Cover Flow view on a 5G iPod nano.

Figure 2.15

Tracks in Cover Flow view on a 5G iPod nano.

Genius (4G iPod nano and iPod classics only)

If you've created a Genius playlist, you'll find it by selecting this command and pressing the Center button. If you haven't created a Genius playlist on your iPod yet, you'll see instructions for how to do so when you execute this command.

Genius Mixes (5G iPod nano only)

iTunes 9 introduced a feature called Genius Mixes. Similar to Genius playlists, Genius Mixes creates 250-track playlists made up of songs organized by genre—Rock, Jazz, and Folk, for example. It works this magic by examining the contents of your iTunes Library, determining the predominant genres in the library, and then creating up to 12 of these large playlists of genre-related tracks.

You have the option to select and sync Genius Mixes to your attached 5G iPod nano within the iTunes Music tab. (As I write these words, the 5G iPod nano and iPod touch are the only iPods that support Genius Mixes.) Do this, and the selected mixes are copied to your iPod and become accessible from the Genius Mixes entry (**Figure 2.16**).

Figure 2.16
A Genius Mix on a 5G iPod nano.

note   You can also access the songs, artists, and albums represented in a
Genius Mix by using the iPod's Song, Artists, and Albums commands.
When you use those methods, however, you won't see the tracks organized by
the mix.

Playlists

Regardless of which iPod you're using, when you choose Playlists and
press the Center button, you'll see a screen that contains the playlists
you've downloaded to your iPod (**Figure 2.17**), as well as any Genius and
On-The-Go playlists you've created on the iPod. Genius playlists are
denoted by the Genius icon next to them. On these iPods, playlists synced
from your computer indicate the number of songs each playlist contains.
Genius playlists don't—and don't need to, as they always contain 25 tracks.

Figure 2.17

*5G iPod nano's
Playlists screen.*

tip   If you've created a folder in iTunes and placed multiple playlists in
that folder, that folder hierarchy is present on the iPod as well. If
I create a folder called Great '50s Jazz and place my Miles Davis, John Coltrane,
and Bill Evans playlists in that folder, when I sync the Great '50s Jazz folder to
my iPod, it appears in the Playlists screen. When I select that folder and press
the Center button, the playlists associated with these jazz greats appear in
the resulting screen.

These playlists are created and configured in iTunes. How you configure them is up to you. You may want to gather all your polka favorites
in one playlist and put ska in another. Or if you have an iPod shared
by the family, Dad may gather his psychedelic songs of the '60s in his
personal playlist, whereas sister Sue creates a playlist full of hip-hop and
house music. When I discuss iTunes in Chapter 4, I'll look at additional
approaches for putting together playlists.

After you select a playlist and press the Center button, the songs within
that playlist appear in a scrollable screen, with the name of the playlist
at the top. Just select the song you want to play and press the Center
button. When you do, you'll move to the Now Playing screen (**Figure 2.18**),
which on the 4G iPod nano displays the name of the song playing and
alternately scrolls the name of the artist and album. Because the iPod
classics and the 5G iPod nano have larger screens, the Now Playing screen
shows the song title, artist, and album without scrolling. The number of
songs in the playlist also appears on the iPod classics.

Figure 2.18
*Now Playing
screen.*

On color iPods and iPod nanos, you'll see a picture of the album cover if
the song has this information embedded in it and iTunes' Display Album
Artwork on Your iPod option is enabled. (Monochrome iPods don't display
album artwork.) Also appearing in this screen are two timer displays:

elapsed time and remaining time. In addition, the screen contains a graphic thermometer display that gives you a visual representation of how far along you are in the song.

note   Text that runs off the screen in the Song, Artist, and Album screens is treated differently on color iPods and the iPod nano from the way it's treated on other iPods. Earlier iPods and the iPod mini place an ellipsis (...) at the end of an entry that exceeds the width of the screen. A color-display iPod or nano, however, scrolls selected text from right to left if the text is longer than the screen can accommodate. It also scrolls text from right to left on the Now Playing screen if the text doesn't fit.

Additional features lie within the Now Playing screen; you reach one of those features by using the click wheel and the others by pressing the Center button.

Change volume. If you turn the click wheel, the timeline at the bottom of the screen shifts off the screen, and a Volume thermometer display appears in its place. Scroll the click wheel clockwise to raise the volume; scroll counterclockwise to lower it.

Scrub music. If you press the Center button while you're in the Now Playing screen, you'll be able to scrub through the song. *Scrubbing* means that you can move back or forward through a track and hear little snippets of the track as you move from place to place. This feature makes it easy to tell where you are in a track. I find it particularly helpful for finding my place in podcasts and audiobooks.

The scrub thermometer display indicates the playing location with a small diamond. Just move your finger across the click wheel to start scrubbing. Stop pushing your digit across the click wheel in either of these screens, and you'll return to the timeline after a couple of seconds.

Recent display-bearing iPods include screens beyond the scrub screen, allowing you to do additional things:

- As I describe earlier in the chapter, when you press the Center button twice, you have the option to invoke the Genius playlist feature (**Figure 2.19**).

Figure 2.19
Now Playing screen's Genius Playlist control.

- Press the Center button three times while you're in the Now Playing screen to go the Ratings screen; then use the click wheel to assign ratings of one to five stars.

- Press the Center button four times, and you arrive at the Shuffle screen, where you find three options: Off, Songs, and Albums. Use the click wheel to move among these options, and press the Center button to select one.

- If you've added lyrics to a track with iTunes 5 or later, pressing the Center button five times in the Now Playing screen takes you to a Lyrics screen.

On-The-Go (Dock-connector iPods)

Scroll to the bottom of the Playlists screen on a Dock-connector iPod, and you'll find an additional playlist that you didn't create: the On-The-Go playlist.

Introduced with iPod Software 2.0 Updater, this playlist is a special one that you create directly on the iPod. It's particularly useful when you want to create a new playlist right now and don't have a computer you can plug your iPod into. It works this way with the 2G iPod classic and the 4G and 5G iPod nanos:

1. Select a song, artist, playlist, album, genre, composer, or compilation.

   In other words, select one of the items available to you in the Music screen.

2. Hold down the Center button.

   On the iPod nano, a sheet appears that includes an Add to On-The-Go command (as well as other commands if you've done this with a track selected, rather than an item like an album that contains multiple tracks). On the 2G iPod classic, you'll see a new screen that contains an Add-to-On-The-Go playlist and, perhaps, those other commands.

3. Select Add-to-On-The-Go, and press Center.

   The iPod returns to the screen it came from, and the item you've added blinks, indicating that it's been added to the On-The-Go playlist.

4. Repeat this procedure for any other items you want to add to the playlist.

5. When you're ready to play your selections, choose On-The-Go from the Playlists screen, and press Center.

   In the resulting On-The-Go screen, you'll see a list of songs you've added to the list, in the order in which you added them. (The song, artist, playlist, or album you selected first appears at the top of the list.)

6. Press the Center button to begin playing the playlist.

To save an On-The-Go playlist, just select Save Playlist in the On-The-Go screen and press the Center button. The first playlist will be called New Playlist 1. After you've saved an On-The-Go playlist, you can create another (and likewise save it). Subsequent saved On-The-Go playlists are numbered in order—New Playlist 2, for example. To clear the On-The-Go playlist, choose Clear Playlist in this same screen, and press the Center button. A confirmation message appears, letting you choose Clear or Cancel (which you select by scrolling the click wheel and then confirm by pressing Center).

On-The-Go playlists for the previous generation of display-bearing iPods work a little differently. To add an item to the On-The-Go playlist, just select it and hold the Center button. The item will blink, which tells you it's been added.

When you synchronize your click-wheel iPod with iTunes, your saved On-The-Go playlists appear successively numbered in iTunes: On-The-Go 1, On-The-Go 2, and (you guessed it) On-The-Go 3, for example. During synchronization, these On-The-Go playlists are removed from the iPod. If you'd like them to remain on the iPod, you must direct iTunes to sync them back to the iPod (more on this in Chapter 4).

Artists

The Artists screen displays the names of all the artists represented on your iPod (**Figure 2.20**). Choose an artist's name and press the Center button, and you'll be transported to that artist's screen. If the tracks listed in that screen are all from the same album, you'll

Figure 2.20

Artists screen.

Artists	‖ ▭
All Albums	›
Alejandro Escovedo	
Alfred Schnittke, Tatja...	
Allman Brothers	
Amos Lee	
Amy Grant	
Antony Pitts	
Apache Beat	
Arts the Beatdoctor	
Arturo Sandoval	
The Association	
Atlanta Symphony Ch...	

see just the track names. If you have tracks from multiple albums by this artist, you can select All Songs—which leads you to a screen that contains a list of all the artist's songs—or you can select albums individually and choose to play just the tracks on a particular album.

You'll also spy the All Albums entry at the top of the Artists screen. Should you choose this entry, you'll be taken to the All Albums screen, where you can select all albums by all artists. The All Albums screen contains an All Songs command of its own. Select this command, and you'll move to the All Songs screen, which lists all songs by all artists on your iPod. (But if a song doesn't have an Artists entry, the song won't appear in this screen.)

Albums

Choose the Albums entry and press the Center button, and you'll see every album represented on your iPod (**Figure 2.21**). Choose an album and press the Center button to play the album from beginning to end. The Albums screen also contains an All Songs entry, which, when selected, displays all the songs on all the albums on your iPod. (If the song doesn't have an Albums entry, it won't appear in this screen.)

Figure 2.21
Albums screen.

note An album entry can contain a single song. As long as the album field has been filled in for a particular song within iTunes or another iPod-compatible application (I discuss this topic in Chapter 4), that song will appear in the Albums screen.

Compilations (iPod classics only)

iTunes and the iPod define *compilation* recordings as those that are part of anthologies and greatest-hits collections. You'd find *Dr. Bobo and the Chiropractic Quintet's 50 Fave Hits* here, as well as the live recording from the Three Days in the Mud and Merriment festival. Only the iPod classics get a Compilations command and screen.

Songs

Choose Songs and press the Center button, and you'll see a list of all the songs on your iPod (**Figure 2.22**).

Figure 2.22

Songs screen.

Genres

The iPod has the capability to sort songs by genre: Acoustic, Blues, Reggae, and Techno, for example. If a song has been tagged with a genre entry, you can choose it by genre in the Genres screen (**Figure 2.23**). On the 3G, 4G, and 5G nanos and iPod classics, below each genre entry you'll see the number of artists and albums that belong to that genre—*6 Artists, 9 Albums,* for example.

Figure 2.23

Genres screen.

Composers

The iPod can also group songs by composers. This feature, added in iPod Software 1.2 Updater, allows you to sort classical music more easily (**Figure 2.24**). In the Composers screen, you'll see an All Albums screen as well as composers' names. Select All Albums and press the Center button, and all the albums that have been tagged with a composer's name will appear in the resulting All Albums screen.

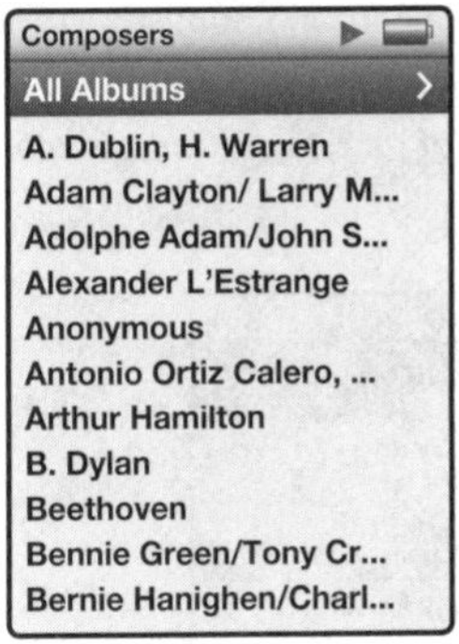

Figure 2.24
Composers screen.

Composers ► ▭
All Albums >
A. Dublin, H. Warren
Adam Clayton/ Larry M...
Adolphe Adam/John S...
Alexander L'Estrange
Anonymous
Antonio Ortiz Calero, ...
Arthur Hamilton
B. Dylan
Beethoven
Bennie Green/Tony Cr...
Bernie Hanighen/Charl...

Audiobooks

The iPod is capable of playing audiobook files purchased from Audible.com and the iTunes Store, as well as audiobooks you've ripped from CDs and tagged as audiobooks (more on this topic in Chapter 4). Audiobooks purchased from Audible.com bear the .aa file extension, and the .m4b extension identifies those bought from the iTunes Store. Audiobooks that you rip yourself can be in any format supported by iTunes (AIFF, WAV, MP3, AAC, or Apple Lossless). When an iPod stores one of these files, the audiobook's name appears in the iPod's Audiobooks screen (which appears when you choose the Audiobooks command in the Music screen and press the Center button).

Search

When Apple released the updated 5G iPod and 2G iPod nano in late 2006, it gave them a new Search feature. Search is also available on the 3G, 4G, and 5G iPod nanos and the iPod classics. Select Search and press the Center button, and you'll see a Search screen. Using the click wheel, you scroll through an alphabetical list. (The 5G iPod's and 2G iPod nano's

Search feature includes both letters and numbers.) When you reach the letter you seek, press the Center button to enter that letter in the Search field. When you do this, a list of matching items appears in the top part of the screen (**Figure 2.25**).

Figure 2.25

Searching for items on the 5G iPod nano.

Continue scrolling and clicking to enter more characters to narrow your search. To remove an unwanted character, press the Previous button to erase the last character you entered. When you've entered as many characters as you care to, select Done on the 5G iPod and 2G iPod nano, and press the Center button. On a 3G, 4G, or 5G nano or iPod classic, just press Menu to exit Search. Doing so takes you to the Search Results screen, where you'll see a list of all albums, artists, and songs containing the character sequence you entered. (Search doesn't work for videos or movies.) Scroll to the item you want, and press the Center button to select it.

If you select a song, it starts playing. If you select an album or artist, you'll see an Albums or Artists screen, and you can continue selecting items and pressing the Center button until you get exactly the track you want.

The Search feature is smarter than you may think. Although the list of results generally begins with the first letter you've entered, that list can also contain entries that contain the letters you've entered within the body of the item. Entering DC, for example, produces not only AC/DC as an artist entry, but also selections that contain the word *podcast*.

All 5G iPods (with the latest iPod software), the 2G–5G iPod nanos, and the iPod classics also support one other kind of searching. Navigate to the Artists, Albums, Songs, or Composers screen, and start scrolling. In short order, a square gray overlay appears in the middle of the screen, including the letter that reflects where you are in the list. If you're scrolling through the Jack Johnson, Jackie Gleason, Jackie Wilson, James Brown, Janis Joplin, and The Jayhawks section of your Artists screen, you'll see the letter *J* overlaid as you scroll.

Videos

Not surprisingly, on traditional iPods, the Videos command is available only on those iPods that are capable of playing video—which, as this book goes to press, are the 5G iPod, the iPod classics, and the 3G–5G iPod nanos. Within the Videos screen (**Figure 2.26**), you'll find the entries that I describe in the following sections.

Figure 2.26

5G iPod nano's Videos screen.

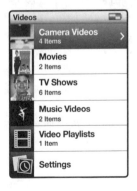

Camera Videos (5G iPod nano only)

By now, you're well aware that the 5G iPod nano carries a video camera. When you record a video with your 5G nano, this entry is where you find it for playback on the iPod. Videos are sorted by the days when they were shot. I discuss the video capabilities of the 5G iPod nano in Chapter 3.

Movies

In iTunes, you can tag a video as a Movie, Music Video, or TV Show (I tell you how in Chapter 4). Any video that has the Movie tag assigned to it will show up in the list that appears when you select Movies in the Videos screen and press the Center button.

Rentals

You can rent movies from the iTunes Store. When you do and then sync them to your iPod, they appear when you select Rentals and press the Center button. I cover movie rentals in Chapter 5.

TV Shows

At the risk of repeating myself, this tag works the same way as the Movie tag. If you have programs tagged as TV Shows, they appear in this list. In the list, you'll see the name of the show and the number of episodes you have on the iPod. Select a show and press the Center button, and you'll see a list of all the show's episodes, complete with episode title and broadcast date. Episodes are sorted from oldest to newest.

Music Videos

This tag works the same way as Movie. Tag a video as a Music Video in iTunes, and it appears in the Music Videos list.

Video Playlists

As I explain in Chapter 4, you can create playlists that contain videos and then copy these playlists (and their contents) to a compatible iPod. When you do, those playlists appear when you select Video Playlists in the Videos screen and press the Center button. Select a playlist and press the button again, and you'll see a list of the videos contained in that playlist. Select an item in the playlist and press the Center button or Play, and the selected video will play.

Settings (Video Settings on 5G iPod, 3G and 4G iPod nanos, and iPod classics)

Select this command in the Videos screen on a 3G, 4G, or 5G nano or iPod classic, and press the Center button to see seven options: TV Out, TV Signal, TV Screen, Fit to Screen, Alternate Audio, Captions, and Subtitles (**Figure 2.27**).

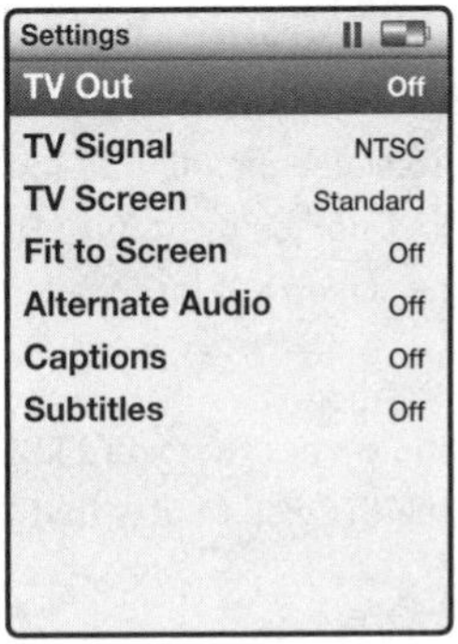

Figure 2.27
*Video Settings
screen.*

Settings	‖ 🔲
TV Out	Off
TV Signal	NTSC
TV Screen	Standard
Fit to Screen	Off
Alternate Audio	Off
Captions	Off
Subtitles	Off

You use TV Out to tell the iPod whether to output its video signal via the headphone port (the 5G iPod outputs video from this port with the assistance of Apple's AV cable) or the Dock-connector port on a 3G, 4G, or 5G iPod nano or iPod classic. Off means no signal. Ask means that when you call up a video on the iPod and press Play to begin the show, a screen will appear, asking you whether you'd like the TV signal turned on or left off. On means that the iPod will automatically send the signal out the Dock-connector port on a 3G, 4G, or 5G iPod nano and iPod classic, and out the headphone port on a 5G iPod.

The world has two major television standards: NTSC (United States and Japan) and PAL (Europe and Australia). You can choose either for your iPod's video output with the TV Out command.

TV Screen tells the iPod what kind of television set you're connecting it to: Standard (4:3) or Widescreen (16:9). The iPod needs to know the TV-screen type so that it can format the video properly. Choose Standard and connect the iPod to a widescreen TV, and you'll see the entire picture, but it will be smaller than what you'd see if you'd chosen Widescreen instead.

Fit to Screen determines both how the video will appear on the iPod's screen as well as on a connected standard-definition TV. Leave this option off, and the video will be letterboxed—meaning that you'll see the entire picture but with black bars above and below it. Turn Fit to Screen on, and the movie will expand to fill the screen but lose the left and right edges of the picture in doing so.

If a movie has an alternative audio track that you'd like to hear (French or Italian, for example), you can tell the iPod to play that track by toggling this option on.

The iPod nanos and iPod classics support closed-captioned videos. As this book goes to press, the iTunes Store sells just under 200 movies with closed captions. If you obtain one of these movies—either through purchase or rental—turning on Captions will allow you to see those movie's captions.

Today's click-wheel iPods can also display subtitles in movies from the iTunes Store that contain subtitles.

note The 5G iPod lists just three commands: TV Out, TV Signal, and Widescreen. The only difference is that Widescreen is the default setting on the 5G iPod. Turning it on displays video in letterbox view; turn it off, and you enter full-screen view.

Photos (color-display iPods only)

The Photos command appears only on iPods with color displays. This command is your avenue for viewing pictures on your iPod, as well as for configuring how slideshows are displayed on it and (if you have a full-size color iPod) on an attached TV set or projector.

At the top of the Photos screen, you'll find an All Photos command. Select it and press the Center button to see thumbnail images of every photo stored on the iPod (**Figure 2.28**). The 4G iPod nano displays 20 thumbnails; the 5G iPod nano, with its larger screen, shows 24 thumbnails; and the classics, 15. Use the click wheel to select an image. When you select an image, the date when it was taken appears at the top of the display

Figure 2.28
Thumbnails in the Photos screen.

on 3G and 4G nanos and iPod classics. No date appears on the 5G iPod nano. To display the image in full-screen view, press the Center button. To move to the next or previous image, press the Next and Previous buttons, respectively, or use the click wheel to move forward or back. To play a slideshow of your images from the point where you selected an image, press the Play/Pause button. To leave the slideshow, press Menu.

The Photos screen also contains a list of any photo albums you've synced to the iPod via iTunes. (I talk about photo albums and iTunes in Chapter 4.) When you select an album on a 3G iPod nano or iPod classic, images from that album swoop across the right side of the split-screen display. The 4G and 5G iPod nanos don't offer this kind of preview of images when you select an album.

Additionally, the Photos screen includes a Settings command. Select it and press the Center button, and you'll see these commands:

Time Per Slide. You can configure the iPod so that slideshows are under manual command, and you need to press the Next or Previous button to navigate the slideshow. You can also have the iPod change slides automatically every 2, 3, 5, 10, or 20 seconds.

Music. Your slideshow can be accompanied by music. In the Slideshow Music screen, choose Now Playing, Off, one of the playlists on the iPod, or the On-The-Go playlist.

Repeat. If you like, you can have your slideshow repeat forever (or at least until the iPod runs out of power). This command is a simple On/Off command.

Shuffle Photos. This command is another On/Off command. Off means that your slides play in order; choose On, and they're displayed randomly.

Transitions. The color iPods offer built-in *transitions* (effects that occur when you move from one slide to another). The included effects on the 3G iPod nano and iPod classics are Random (a random mix of effects), Cross Fade, Fade to Black, Zoom Out, Wipe Across, and Wipe Center. The 4G iPod nano includes Random, Dissolve, Slide, Push, Fade Through Black, and Zoom transitions. The 5G iPod nano offers Random, Dissolve, Cube, Ken Burns, Flip, and Push. The 5G iPod offers a broader set of transitions, including Random, Cube Across, Cube Down, Dissolve, Page Flip, Push Across, Push Down, Radial, Swirl, Wipe Across, Wipe Down, and Wipe from Center.

TV Out (including the 5G iPod, 3G–5G iPod nanos, and iPod classics). This command works just as it does for video settings.

 Turning on TV output depletes the battery charge in a big way. Switch this option on only if you really need it.

TV Signal (including the 5G iPod, 3G–5G iPod nanos, and iPod classics). Same here: Your options are NTSC and PAL.

Photo Import (full-size color iPods before the iPod classics). Full-size color iPods produced before the iPod classics can import photos from many digital cameras, using Apple's now-discontinued $29 iPod Camera Connector. When you connect a supported camera to your iPod via this device, the Photo Import command appears in the Photos screen. Click it, and you'll find a list of all the rolls (import sessions) for photos you've brought into the iPod. The iPod classics and 3G, 4G, and 5G iPod nanos are not compatible with this accessory.

Podcasts (click-wheel iPods only)

As you likely know, *podcasts* are Internet broadcasts that you download and place on your iPod for later listening. Podcasts downloaded through

the iTunes Store are routed to your iPod and placed under this heading on click-wheel iPods (**Figure 2.29**). On earlier iPods, you'll find the
Podcasts entry in the Playlists screen.

Figure 2.29

Podcasts screen.

If you've listened to podcasts on older iPods, you should be aware of this
convenient feature. When you play an episode of a podcast on a 3G nano
or iPod classic, when the episode concludes, the iPod immediately plays
the next episode, if there is one (starting with the most recent episode
and then playing the next most recent). On older iPods and, inexplicably,
the 4G and 5G nanos, at the conclusion of the episode you're taken back
to the Podcasts screen. This "keep on keepin' on" feature is useful when
you're listening to a podcast in your car—and safer, too. No longer do you
have to take your eyes off the road to listen to another episode of your
favorite podcast.

Radio

The 5G iPod nano has a built-in FM radio. Choose this command, and
you'll see the station the iPod is currently tuned to. I discuss this radio
in detail in Chapter 3.

Video Camera

This feature, introduced with the 5G iPod nano, also gets its due in Chapter 3.

Extras

The Extras screen is the means to all the iPod's nonmusical functions—its contacts, calendars, clock, and games. Here's what you'll find for each entry.

Alarms

When you select Alarms and press the Center button, you'll see the Alarms screen, which has at least two entries: Create Alarm and Sleep Timer. If you've created any events in your computer's calendar program that have alarms attached to them, those events appear in this screen as well (**Figure 2.30**).

Figure 2.30
Alarms synced from iCal.

Alarms	❚❚ ▭
Create Alarm New Alarm	>
Sleep Timer Inactive	
Lunch with Kathy 12:00 PM	
Rob Video 11:50 PM	
Dan F. Video 11:50 PM	
Roman Video 11:50 PM	
Jason Video 11:50 PM	

To create a new alarm, select Create Alarm and press the Center button. In the resulting screen, you'll see the option to turn the alarm on or off, as well as entries for Date, Time, Repeat, Alert (4G and 5G iPod nanos) or Sound (iPod classics), Label, and Delete.

Select Date and press the Center button, and the Alarms screen appears. You can enter dates by using the click wheel to scroll through the month, day, and year fields and pressing the Next and Previous buttons to move from one field to the next. The Time entry works very much the same way.

Repeat allows you to choose how often the alarm occurs. You can select Once, Every Day, Weekdays, Weekends, Every Week, Every Month, or Every Year.

Alert (4G and 5G iPod nanos)/Sounds (iPod classics) lets you choose Tones (None, which displays just a visual alarm, or Beep, which displays that visual alarm *and* causes the iPod to beep) or Playlists. When you choose Playlists and press the Center button, you can choose a playlist to play when the alarm goes off. This option is useful if your iPod is plugged into a speaker system or an iPod-compatible alarm clock.

A Label feature that appears for the first time on today's traditional iPods lets you choose one of 23 labels for your alarm, including Wake Up, Work, Party, Anniversary, and Take Medicine.

Finally, you can undo the alarm you're creating by scrolling down to Delete and pressing the Center button.

When an alarm goes off, a visual alarm appears that details the alarm— the time, date, and label. In this screen, you can choose to dismiss the alarm or snooze.

note The Sleep Timer entry in the Alarms screen is for all those who like to fall asleep to music. Just plug your iPod into a speaker system (or wear headphones, I suppose, if you don't mind sleeping with them on), start it playing, and set a sleep timer (Off or 15, 30, 60, 90, or 120 minutes). The iPod will play for the time indicated; then it, too, will go to sleep.

note The order of commands in the Extras screen is different for the 4G iPod nano, 5G iPod nano, and the iPod classics. The 4G nano lists Alarms, Calendars, Clocks, Contacts, Games, Notes, Screen Lock, and Stopwatch. The 5G iPod nano includes Alarms, Calendars, Clocks, Contacts, Fitness, Games, Notes, Screen Lock, Stopwatch, and Voice Memos. The iPod classics list Clocks, Calendars, Contacts, Alarms, Games, Notes, Screen Lock, and Stopwatch. I've opted to use the order listed on the 5G iPod nano, as it's the more popular device.

Calendars

I also address calendar creation later in the book, so for now, just know that when you select the Calendars entry on one of today's click-wheel iPods, you'll see, at the very least, an All Calendars entry, To Do's, and Alarms. If you've created multiple calendars in an application such as Apple's iCal, you see separate calendar entries if you've asked iTunes to sync individual calendars (see Chapter 6).

When you select All Calendars and press the Center button, the current month is displayed in a window with the current day highlighted. If a day has an event attached to it, that day displays a small red flag on the 5G iPod, the iPod classics, and all iPod nanos except the 4G and 5G iPod nanos, which display a small black dot. (Earlier iPods display events as small black rectangles.) The 3G iPod nano and iPod classics place small bell icons on days that include an alarm. The 4G and 5G iPod nanos don't include this bell icon but list any events for the selected day at the bottom of the screen. That list includes the time of the event and its title—*9:00 AM–10:30 AM Meeting with Curly*, for example (**Figure 2.31** on the next page).

Use the click wheel to move to a different day; scroll forward to look into the future; and scroll back to be transported back in time. To jump to the next or previous month, press the Next or Previous button, respectively. When you want to see the details of an event, scroll to its day and press the Center button. Any events scheduled for that day will appear in the

Figure 2.31

Calendars screen.

resulting screen. You can move to the next or previous day by pressing Next and Previous, respectively. Select an event and press the Center button, and you'll see any details attached to the event—the date, time, location, and any notes you've added, for example.

The To Do's entry is for any to-do items you've created in your computer's calendar application. A To Do's screen will give you a summary of the item (Finish the Book!, for example); its priority (hot items are given a priority of 1); and a due date, if you've created one. Notes are not included. You can move among To Do items in this Summary screen by pressing the Next and Previous buttons.

Finally, selecting Alarms and pressing the Center button cycles the options through Off, Beep, and None. Off means that the iPod won't alert you to alarms. Beep indicates that the iPod will produce an audible beep. Setting the iPod to None activates a visual alert but no audible alarm.

Clocks

Yes, the iPod can tell time. Clicking Clocks displays the current time and date on today's click-wheel iPods. The top of the Clocks screen displays both an analog and a digital clock (**Figure 2.32**).

Figure 2.32
Clocks screen.

You can add clocks or edit the selected clock by pressing the Center button. When you do, a small bar appears that includes the words *Add*, *Edit*, and *Delete* (when you've added a clock), with Add selected by default. Press the Center button again, and a Region screen appears. Choose a region with the click wheel, press the Center button, and choose a city in the resulting City screen to create a clock that reflects the time in that city.

When you choose Edit, you can choose a new region and city for that clock. Choosing Delete removes the selected clock. (If you have just one clock on the screen, though, it can't be removed.)

Contacts

I also discuss how to create contacts in Chapter 6. In the meantime, you need to know only that to access your contacts, you choose Contacts in the Extras screen and press the Center button. On all click-wheel iPods save the 4G and 5G iPod nanos, scroll through your list of contacts and press the button again to view the information within a contact. If a contact contains more information than will fit in the display, use the click wheel to scroll down the window.

On the 4G and 5G iPod nanos, any groups you've created will appear in a Contract Group screen when you select Contacts and press the Center button. Then you can select a group, press the Center button, and view just the contacts in that group.

If you haven't placed any contacts on your 3G iPod nano or iPod classic, when you select Contacts in the Extras screen, the right side of the display reads *No Contacts*. If you press the Center button at this point, nothing happens. Select Contacts on a 4G or 5G iPod nano and press the Center button when you have no contacts on the iPod, and you see a screen that reads *No* Contacts.

On earlier iPods, clicking the Contacts entry with no contacts on the iPod reveals two entries in the Contacts screen: Instructions and Sample. You can probably guess that selecting Instructions provides directions on how to move contacts to your iPod. The Sample command shows you what a complete contact looks like.

Fitness (5G iPod nano)

The 5G iPod nano has a pedometer feature that counts the steps you take. Fitness is another of those 5G iPod nano features that I discuss in the next chapter.

Games

The 3G iPod nano and iPod classics include three games: iQuiz, Klondike, and Vortex. To play one of them, just select Games, press the Center button, select the game, and press that button once again. The 4G and 5G iPod nanos replace iQuiz with Maze, a game that takes advantage of the iPods' accelerometer. The games work this way:

iQuiz. As its name implies, iQuiz is a quiz-show kind of game. By default, you have a choice of four quizzes: Music Quiz 2, Movie Trivia, Music Trivia, and TV Show Trivia. Music Quiz 2 uses music stored on your iPod as the basis of its questions (**Figure 2.33**). It may play a tune, for example, and ask you whether such-and-such a title is correct. Answer yes or no by using the click wheel and Center button. Movie Trivia, Music Trivia, and TV Show Trivia use prepackaged questions and answers contained on the iPod. For all questions, you have about 15 seconds to answer.

Figure 2.33
iQuiz game.

 You can create your own games for iQuiz. Apple tells you how at www. apple.com/games/ipod/iquiz.

Klondike. Klondike is the classic solitaire game (**Figure 2.34**). To play, arrange alternating colors of cards in descending sequence—a sequence that could run jack of hearts, 10 of spades, 9 of diamonds, 8 of clubs, and so on—in the bottom portion of the screen. In the top portion of the window, you arrange cards in an ascending sequence of the same suit—ace, 2, 3, 4, and 5 of hearts, for example.

Figure 2.34
Klondike game.

Use the click wheel to move the hand pointer to the card you want to move. Press the Center button to select a card that you want to place somewhere and the logical destination for it is highlighted (for example, you choose an ace, and one of the four spaces at the top of the display lights up). Press the Center button again, and the card moves to that place.

On the 4G and 5G iPod nanos, this game plays in landscape mode, meaning that you have to turn the iPod on its side to play the game.

Vortex. This game is a bit like the arcade game Breakout (or Brick), in which you bounce a ball off a wall to break down a barrier (**Figure 2.35**). In this case, the wall is round, and your paddle rotates around the outside of the wall. Press the Center button to unleash the ball, and control the paddle with the click wheel.

Figure 2.35
Vortex game.

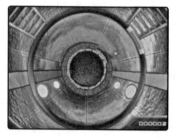

On the 4G and 5G iPod nanos, you can play this game in either orientation—landscape or portrait.

 Apple sells games made for recent click-wheel iPods at the App Store. These games include such perennials as Monopoly, Yahtzee, Bejeweled, and Pac-Man. The 4G and 5G iPod nanos play these games in landscape mode, which seemingly makes the controls unintuitive. You may think you have to continue to press Menu to go up, even though the Menu button is now on the left. Don't worry—when you rotate the iPod, the orientation of the controls changes as well, so that Menu and Play/Pause become left and right, respectively. The nano displays a screen before these games start to familiarize you with these changes (**Figure 2.36**).

Figure 2.36
The game-control diagram on the 5G iPod nano.

Maze. This 4G and 5G iPod–only game uses the iPod's accelerometer to nice effect. Similar to the wooden labyrinth games of days gone by, Maze demands that you tilt the iPod to guide a virtual metal ball through a series of mazes, picking up bonuses along the way by rolling over them as well as avoiding traps by maneuvering around them (**Figure 2.37**).

Figure 2.37
Maze game.

Notes

Notes allows you to store text files (up to 4 KB, or 4,096 characters) on your iPod. To add notes to your iPod, mount the iPod on your computer (the iPod must be configured to appear on the desktop), double-click the iPod to reveal its contents, and drag a text file into the iPod's Notes folder. When you unmount your iPod, you'll find the name of your text file in the Notes area of the Extras screen. The 1G and 2G iPods don't have this function.

Screen Lock

Screen Lock is a feature for . . . well, locking your iPod's screen. Like a cheap bike lock, this lock lets you create a four-digit password by using numbers from 0 through 9. The interface on the 5G iPod and the 1G and 2G nanos features a round combination wheel with four digits above it. The 3G, 4G, and 5G nanos and iPod classics place the four digits in a row (**Figure 2.38**). To move from one digit to another, press the Next and Previous buttons. Pressing the Center button also takes you to the next digit and, when you reach the final digit, sets the code. You'll be asked to confirm the combination by entering it again. A lock icon will appear when the iPod is locked. To unlock it, press the Center button and enter the combination when prompted.

Figure 2.38

Screen Lock.

Stopwatch

The Stopwatch tracks total time and lap time. Choose Stopwatch and click the Center button to be taken to the Stopwatch screen. The first time you use the stopwatch on a 3G, 4G, or 5G iPod nano or iPod classic, you'll see a picture of a stopwatch with a Play/Pause button next to it. Press the Center button to start the timer (**Figure 2.39**).

Figure 2.39
Stopwatch.

Each time you press the Center button as the timer runs, a lap time is added to the screen, as well as to a timer log. (An iPod classic's screen can display up to three lap times along with the current timer; the 4G and 5G iPod nanos display two lap times.) To pause the stopwatch, just press the Play/Pause button. You can keep the timer running by pressing the Menu button.

When you press that Menu button on an iPod classic or a 3G iPod nano, the Stopwatch screen splits so that the stopwatch is on the right and a list of commands is on the left. This list includes Resume, which takes you back to the full-screen view of the timer; New Timer, for creating a new timer and saving the previous timer to the timer log; Clear Logs, which deletes any logs saved on the iPod; Current Log, which shows you the statistics for the current log (including the date, the time, and the short-est, longest, and average lap times); and then a list of any logs you've saved. Similar to the Current Log, these logs include date, time, and lap data. The 4G and 5G iPod nanos' screens, being smaller, don't split. Instead, you're taken to a separate Stopwatch screen.

Nike + iPod (iPod nano only)

This command appears only if you've plugged the Nike + Sport Kit receiver into your iPod nano's Dock-connector port. It leads to a Workout screen that allows you to choose among four main options: Basic, Time, Distance, and Calories. Within a Settings screen, you'll also find menu options for PowerSong (one track you've chosen that will activate with the press of the Center button at a key point of your workout); Spoken Feedback (choose a male or a female voice to issue feedback); Distances (miles or kilometers); and Sensor, where you calibrate the Sport Kit for your body.

Voice Memos

Late-model full-size iPods and the 2G, 3G, and 4G iPod nanos can record voice memos with a compatible microphone adapter. The 5G iPod nano can record these memos with its built-in microphone. When you plug such an adapter into an iPod classic or a 3G or 4G iPod nano, this command appears in the iPod's Mail screen. On the 5G iPod nano, this command is located in the Extras screen.

The 4G iPod nano and 2G iPod classic can also record voice memos with a compatible microphone plugged into the headphone port. Apple sells such a compatible microphone as part of its $29 Apple Earphones with Remote and Mic—a variation on the iPhone headphones bundled with these iPods that contains a headphone control complete with microphone. Again, because the 5G iPod nano has a built-in microphone, you don't need a special set of headphones to record audio. I discuss more of the specifics of the 5G iPod nano's audio-recording capabilities in Chapter 3.

Regardless of where you find this command on your iPod, press the Center button, and you're taken to the Voice Memos screen, where you can choose to record a new voice memo or play back memos you've already recorded. When you sync your iPod with iTunes, your recordings are transferred to a Voice Memos playlist in iTunes' Source list. During the process, the memos are removed from the iPod.

Settings

The Settings screen (**Figure 2.40**) is the path to your iPod preferences—including backlight timer and startup-volume settings, EQ selection, and the language that the iPod displays. The Settings screens of the 4G iPod nano, 5G iPod nano, and iPod classics differ in a few ways; I'll point out where they do. The following sections look at these settings individually.

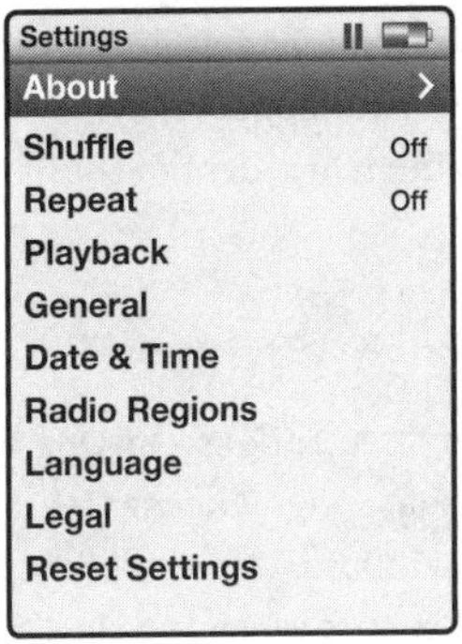

Figure 2.40
5G iPod nano's Settings screen.

Settings	❚❚ ▭
About	**›**
Shuffle	Off
Repeat	Off
Playback	
General	
Date & Time	
Radio Regions	
Language	
Legal	
Reset Settings	

About

Select About and press the Center button once, and you see a graphic display similar to iTunes' Capacity bar that provides details about the iPod's storage and how it's being used. Here, you'll learn how much space has been used and how much remains, as well as get a general notion of how much of your storage is devoted to audio, video, photos, and data.

For a much more specific idea of what's on your iPod, press the Center button again. In the next screen, you see exactly how many songs, videos, podcasts, photos, games, and contacts your iPod holds. Press the Center button one more time, and you'll see your iPod's serial number, model number, and software version.

 You can also press the Next and Previous buttons to move through these screens.

Shuffle

Selecting Shuffle and pressing the Center button rotates you through three settings: Off, Songs, and Albums. When Shuffle is set to Off, the iPod plays the songs in a playlist in the order in which they appear onscreen. The Songs setting plays all the songs within a selected playlist or album in random order. If no album or playlist is selected, the iPod plays all the songs on the iPod in random order. And the Albums setting plays the songs within each album in order but shuffles the order in which the albums are played.

Repeat

The Repeat setting also offers three options: Off, One, and All. When you choose Off, the iPod won't repeat songs. Choose One, and you'll hear the selected song play repeatedly. Choose All, and all the songs within the selected playlist or album will repeat when the playlist or album has played all the way through. If you haven't selected a playlist or album, all the songs on the iPod will repeat after they've played through.

Playback (4G and 5G iPod nanos only)

The 4G and 5G iPod nanos carry a Playback command, which gathers together many of the iPod's music functions. Select Playback and press the Center button, and you'll see the commands shown in **Figure 2.41**.

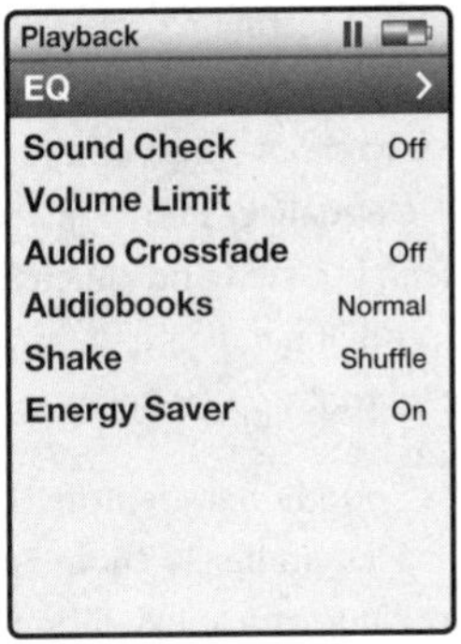

Figure 2.41
*5G iPod nano's
Playback screen.*

Playback	⏸ 🔋
EQ	❯
Sound Check	Off
Volume Limit	
Audio Crossfade	Off
Audiobooks	Normal
Shake	Shuffle
Energy Saver	On

EQ. *EQ* (or *equalization*) is the process of boosting or cutting certain frequencies in the audio spectrum—making the low frequencies louder and the high frequencies quieter, for example. If you've ever adjusted the bass and treble controls on your home or car stereo, you get the idea.

The iPod comes with the same EQ settings as iTunes:

- Off
- Bass Booster
- Classical
- Deep
- Flat
- Jazz
- Loudness
- Piano
- R & B
- Small Speakers
- Treble Booster
- Vocal Booster
- Acoustic
- Bass Reducer
- Dance
- Electronic
- Hip Hop
- Latin
- Lounge
- Pop
- Rock
- Spoken Word
- Treble Reducer

Although you can listen to each EQ setting to get an idea of what it does, you may find it easier to open iTunes; choose Window > Equalizer; and, in the resulting Equalizer window, choose the various EQ settings from the window's pop-up menu. The equalizer's ten band sliders will show you which frequencies have been boosted and which have been cut. Any slider that appears above the 0 dB line indicates a frequency that has been boosted. Conversely, sliders that appear below 0 dB have been cut.

Sound Check. iTunes includes a Sound Check feature that you use to make the volumes of all your tracks similar. Without Sound Check, you may be listening to a Chopin prelude at a lovely, lilting volume and be scared out of your socks when the next track, AC/DC's "Highway to Hell," blasts through your brain. When Sound Check is on, each track should be closer to the same relative volume.

The iPod includes an On/Off Sound Check option, but it works only if you've first switched Sound Check on in iTunes; iTunes must evaluate your tracks and set an instruction in each one so that all the tracks work with Sound Check. To enable Sound Check in iTunes, open iTunes' Preferences, click the Playback icon, and enable the Sound Check option. Now when you sync your tracks with the iPod and switch Sound Check on in the iPod's Music settings screen, you'll experience all that is Sound Check.

Volume Limit. This feature was added in the middle of 2006 at the request of parents who were afraid that their kids would blow out their eardrums by playing music at too high a volume. On the 3G, 4G, and 5G iPod nanos and iPod classics, select Volume Limit and press the Center button, and you'll see a volume thermometer. Use the click wheel to adjust the peak volume (indicated by a small triangle) up or down. Press the Center button to set the volume limit, and you're taken to a screen where you can choose to lock the limit with a four-digit passcode or click Done to impose the limit without a passcode.

Audio Crossfade. Audio Crossfade is a feature introduced with the 4G iPod nano and also available on the 5G iPod nano. Switch it on if you want the end of each track to fade out and the beginning of the next track to fade in.

Audiobooks. One unique feature of the click-wheel iPods is their ability to slow or speed the playback of audiobooks without changing the pitch of the narrator. When you select Audiobooks and press the Center button on your 3G, 4G, or 5G iPod nano or your iPod classic, you cycle through three choices: Slower, Normal, and Faster. The Slower and Faster commands slow or speed playback by about 25 percent, respectively.

You're likely thinking that it would take a minor miracle to pull this trick off without making the book sound odd. You're right; it would. And so far, Apple has failed to achieve this miracle. When you slow down an audio-book, the resulting audio sounds like it was recorded in a particularly reverberant bathroom; you hear a very short echo after each word. Files that are speeded up appear to have lost all the spaces between words, making the book sound as though it's being read by an overcaffeinated auctioneer.

Shake. Shake is another feature that's unique to the 4G and 5G iPod nanos. If, while listening to music on this nano, you want to change to Shuffle mode and play tracks randomly, just give the nano a good shake. (I mean a pretty severe shake. Apple engineered the nano so that the shaking generated by even vigorous exercise doesn't throw the iPod into Shuffle mode.) Shake is an On/Off command. You can choose Shuffle (On) or Off. (You can shake it all you like, and nothing results other than a possibly sore wrist.)

Energy Saver. This feature is yet another that's unique to 4G and 5G nanos. Switch on this On/Off feature, and the nano's display goes dark if you're not using the controls. Yes, the Backlight setting should take care of this situation, but if you've configured the backlight to always be on, switching Energy Saver on will dim the screen regardless of what the Backlight setting says.

General (4G and 5G iPod nanos only)

Just as Apple created a menu command to encompass the 4G and 5G iPod nanos' music commands, it created the General command to pull together the iPod's interface settings (**Figure 2.42**).

Figure 2.42
5G iPod nano's
General screen.

General	II
Clicker	On
Rotate	Cover Flow
Spoken Menus	Off
Backlight	
Brightness	
Font Size	Standard
Main Menu	
Music Menu	
Sort Contacts	Last

The settings work like this:

Clicker. This option makes your iPod's click-wheel actually click—a handy option when you're scrolling through your iPod without looking at it. Clicker provides audible feedback when, for example, you're trying to move to the next command or playlist while driving. Recent click-wheel iPods allow you only to turn the clicker on and off. When the clicker is on, the click sound plays both through the headphones and through the iPod's tiny internal speaker.

Rotate. When your iPod displays the Main or Music menu (or items within the Music-menu hierarchy), and you turn your iPod nano on its side, Cover Flow view appears. If you'd rather that it didn't, just choose Rotate and click the Center button so that option reads Off.

Spoken Menus. Imagine being visually impaired or blind and trying to use a display-bearing iPod. Before the 4G iPod nano, doing that was nigh-on impossible. With that 4G nano, however, Apple brought far greater accessibility to the nano line with Spoken Menus. The command does exactly what it suggests. When Spoken Menus is switched on in both iTunes (in the iPod's Summary tab) and on the iPod, the iPod will speak the name of any highlighted item, including commands, playlists, albums, artists, and tracks.

note The voice you hear depends on the kind of computer you sync the iPod to. If you're using a Mac, by default you'll hear Mac OS X's Alex voice. (You also have the option to choose the system voice that you've selected in the Speech system preference's Text to Speech tab. On a Windows PC, you hear a more "computery" voice.

Although the 5G iPod nano maintains this feature, you have an additional way to make the nano speak to you. In iTunes 9 and later, you have the option to enable VoiceOver separately from Spoken Menus. Enable this feature in iTunes and sync your 5G iPod nano; thereafter, whenever you press the Center button while a track is playing, the iPod will announce the name and artist of that track. This feature is helpful when you're driving with an iPod and don't want to take your eyes off the road to learn the title and artist of a playing track.

Backlight. The iPod's backlight pulls its power from the battery, and when backlighting is left on for very long, it significantly shortens the time you can play your iPod on a single charge. For this reason, Apple includes a timer that automatically switches off backlighting after a certain user-configurable interval. You set that interval by choosing the Backlight setting (called Backlight Timer on earlier iPods).

On iPods before the color iPods, the settings available to you are Off, 2 Seconds, 5 Seconds, 10 Seconds, 20 Seconds, 30 Seconds, and (for those who give not a whit about battery life or who are running the iPod from the Apple Power Adapter) Always On.

Brightness. Today's traditional display-bearing iPods carry a Brightness setting. Select it and press the Center button, and you can dial your iPod's brightness up or down.

Font Size. You won't find this command on other iPods. Because the 4G and 5G iPod nanos' screens are on the small side, Apple tried to do something for those of us who have to squint at the standard font size. Using this command, you can toggle between Standard and Large font sizes. This setting affects menu commands only. Text in the Now Playing screen, for example, doesn't change.

Main Menu. The Main Menu command offers you a way to customize what you see in the iPod's main screen. Choose Main Menu and press the Center button. In the resulting screen, you can choose to view a host of commands. To enable or disable a command, press the Center button to toggle the command on or off. To return the main menu to its default setting, choose the Reset Menu command, press the Center button, choose Reset in the Reset Menus screen, and press the button again. The one unique command in this screen is Preview Panel. Select it and click the Center button so that it reads Off, and you won't see artwork or information in the nano's main screen.

Music Menu. This menu works just like the Main Menu command. The difference is that the commands in this screen apply to the Music menu. The menu also includes a Reset Menu entry.

Sort Contacts. You use this command to choose whether to sort contacts stored on the iPod by first or last name.

Date & Time

The Date & Time command is your means of setting the time zone that your iPod inhabits, as well as the current date and time. In the Date & Time screen, you'll find these options:

Date. Click this command, and in the resulting screen, you'll see a numeric display of the date, including fields for month, date, and year. Move among these fields by pressing the Next and Previous buttons, and increase or decrease their values with the click wheel. Press Menu when you're done.

Time. This screen is very similar to the Date screen. You use the click wheel to change the hour, minutes, AM/PM, date, month, and year values, and use the Forward and Previous buttons to move from value to value.

Time Zone. On the 3G–5G nanos and iPod classics, the Time Zone screen displays a map of the world. Use the click wheel to increment or decrement time. As you do, a red pushpin icon that represents the current time zone moves to the location of major cities within the current time zone.

Setting the time zone on a 5G iPod isn't nearly as much fun. The Time Zone screen on this iPod simply provides a list of major world cities. Select the one that represents your time zone, and press the Menu button.

24 Hour Clock. If you're fond of military or international time (or if you just like saying "Fourteen hundred hours, sir!" in a commanding voice), this option is for you. It allows the iPod to keep time by using either a 12- or 24-hour clock.

Time in Title. This command allows the iPod to display the time in the iPod's title bar.

Radio Regions (5G iPod nano only)

FM frequencies are different around the world. In the United States, we tune a radio from 87.5 to 107.9, but in Japan, these frequencies run from 76.0 to 90.0. Having the option to choose among the world's five regions—Americas, Asia, Australia, Europe, and Japan—makes the 5G iPod nano a terrific international companion that's radio-compatible regardless of which country you're visiting.

Language

The 3G and 4G iPod nano and the iPod classics can display 22 languages (earlier iPods display 21 languages). The 5G iPod nano displays 30 languages. Here's where you set which language your iPod will show.

Legal

If you care to view a few copyright notices, feel free to choose the Legal setting and press the Center button.

Reset Settings

As the name implies, selecting Reset Settings, using the click wheel to select Reset, and pressing the Center button will reset settings to their default. Your iPod's music will stay right where it is; this command just restores the interface to the way it was when the iPod came out of the box.

---

iPod classic Settings Commands

OK, just what you iPod classic owners have been waiting for: the complete list of iPod classic Settings commands!

I'm sorry to disappoint you, but I've covered nearly all of them. The 4G and 5G iPod nanos simply place most of these commands in the Playback and General menus. iPod classic Settings commands run in this order: About, Shuffle, Repeat, Main Menu, Music Menu, Volume Limit, Backlight, Brightness, Audiobooks, EQ, Sound Check, Clicker, Date & Time, Sort By (performs the same duty as the nano's Sort Contacts command), Language, Legal, and Reset Settings.

Shuffle Songs

You may think that choosing this option causes the iPod to play all the material it contains in random order. Not exactly. Shuffle Songs changes the iPod's behavior based on the Shuffle setting in the Settings screen. It works this way:

If you press Shuffle Songs when Shuffle is set to Off or to Songs, the iPod will play songs at random. (Note that it won't play any files it recognizes as audiobooks.)

If you press Shuffle Songs when Shuffle is set to Albums, the iPod picks an album at random and then plays the songs on that album in succession (the order in which they appear on the album). When that album finishes playing, the iPod plays a different album.

If you also switch the Repeat command in the Settings menu to All and press Shuffle Songs, the iPod plays through all the songs on the iPod in the order determined by the Shuffle command and then repeats them in the same order in which they were shuffled originally. If you have three songs on your iPod—A, B, and C—and the iPod shuffles them to be in B, C, A order, when they repeat, they'll repeat as B, C, and A. The iPod won't reshuffle them.

Now Playing

When you select Now Playing, you'll see the name of the currently playing (or paused) track. On an iPod classic, this name appears on the right side of the split-screen display. If you have the Preview Panel enabled on your 4G iPod nano, you'll see the song title at the bottom of the screen. Press the Center button, and you're taken to the Now Playing screen.

3

5G iPod nano Special Features

Descendant of the midpriced, modestly capable, and highly popular iPod mini, the iPod nano inherited each of these traits. It cost less than the capacious full-size iPod and more than the limited iPod shuffle; it had just enough features to make it a capable music player, but not much more; and its svelte design made it a popular choice for those who desired a screen-bearing iPod but didn't want or need a full-size iPod.

With the third generation of this iPod, Apple did something unexpected: It brought every important feature of the full-size iPod of the time (the 5G iPod) to the iPod nano. Unless you really needed the higher capacity of the full-size iPod to hold a large media collection, or you just couldn't bear to watch video on the nano's small screen, the midsize iPod was your meat.

Proving that these benefits weren't due to a slip-up at the head office, Apple gave the 4G iPod nano features that weren't available on the full-size iPod, such as an accelerometer and Spoken Menus. Now, with the 5G iPod nano—which offers a video camera, integrated microphone, FM radio, and pedometer—Apple has pretty well indicated that those who want the fullest-featured click-wheel iPod will eschew the iPod classics and instead look to the nano.

In this chapter, I examine the 5G iPod nano's special talents.

Video Camera

You've heard of this YouTube thing, yes? You know about this Internet-based place to share videos you've produced with the rest of the world, right? It turns out that people—young people in particular—like nothing better than feeding this beast and services similar to it. Whether the filmed content is an aspiring musician in her bedroom crooning a song she's written, a daredevil on his skateboard trying (and failing) to leap over 17 burros, or the foot-in-mouth pronouncement of a soon-to-be-unemployed politician, it's all ripe for YouTube.

To cash in on the public's desire to feed YouTube and other video sharing services, a variety of companies have found ways to bring inexpensive video capture to the masses. Some—such as Pure Digital, Kodak, and Creative Technology—have developed easy-to-use pocket camcorders. Others have incorporated video cameras into existing devices such as point-and-shoot cameras, mobile phones, and music players.

With the iPhone 3GS, Apple jumped on this bandwagon by allowing its latest iPhone to shoot not only still images, but also standard-definition video. The 5G iPod nano is the second Apple media device to shoot video.

note The 5G iPod nano shoots video only—no stills—because Apple claims that the circuitry necessary for shooting decent still images is too thick for the nano's thin design. How thick would it have to be? The iPhone's camera (which can take still images) is about 6 mm thick, whereas the 5G nano's video camera (meaning the sensor and surrounding circuits) is just 3 mm thick. The thickest part of the whole nano is just 6.2 mm.

Speaking of specs

Unlike the majority of today's pocket camcorders (and many new point-and-shoot cameras), the 5G iPod nano shoots standard-definition video (640 by 480 pixels) rather than 720p (1280 by 720 pixels) high-definition video. It encodes video by using the H.264 scheme—a variant of MPEG-4 video that produces good results at low bit rates. And speaking of encoders and bit rates . . .

Of Encoders and Bit Rates

How can an iPod as tiny as the nano capture hours of video? It does this with the help of something called a *codec* (short for *c*ompressor/ *de*compressor). A codec is a bit of technology that compresses (encodes) and decompresses (decodes) data. In the case of the 5G iPod nano, the codec is termed *lossy* because, to make smaller files, it has to perform several tricks to strip out data that you're less likely to miss in the resulting video. The 5G iPod nano (like the iPhone 3GS and nearly all of today's pocket camcorders, for that matter) uses a variant of the MPEG-4 video codec called *H.264*. The H.264 codec produces very nice results at low bit rates, which is why you see it used increasingly in pocket camcorders as well as on Web sites such as YouTube and Vimeo that stream both standard- and high-definition video.

(continued on next page)

Of Encoders and Bit Rates (continued)

Average bit rate is the average amount of data transferred within a particular period. The amount of data (video) captured with a video camera is measured in megabits (millions of bits) per second. You can broadly say that the higher the bit rate, the better the video looks (and the larger the file is), *with this caveat:* You can't compare the performance of one codec with another based solely on bit rate. As I just mentioned, the H.264 codec performs very well at even low bit rates. MPEG-4 video at that same low bit rate could look terrible in comparison.

Reality-checking expectations and results

When Steve Jobs introduced the 5G iPod nano in September 2009, he made it clear where the nano's video camera fit in the scheme of things by displaying a picture of Pure Digital's popular Flip Ultra pocket camcorder. Here, he said, is a device that holds 4 GB of flash memory, costs $150, and *only* shoots video (oh, and look how thick it is). The 5G iPod nano holds twice the memory for the same price and is not only a video camera, but also a darned fine media player.

What Jobs didn't do was compare the quality of the video recorded by these devices—and that's probably for the best, as the 5G nano's video camera doesn't perform as well as the Flip Ultra. There's only so much that a 3mm camera circuit can do. In this case, only so much means that the nano's outside shots are a little dark; its inside shots are also dark, with a lot of artifacts; and just about everything it captures has a blue hue. Also, like all pocket camcorders, this one lacks image stabilization, meaning that you'll see a fair amount of camera shake unless you hold the device very steady. In addition, the nano lacks any variety of zoom and doesn't have a flash. In short, its camera isn't the one you'll use to create your next big-budget movie or music video.

The nano's camera can, however, be the one you'll use to capture any spontaneous moment, because the camera you have with you captures the world around you far better than no camera at all. If the moment—rather than how the moment looks—is what's important to you, the 5G iPod nano's camera is fine. That said, if you also happen to have a dedicated pocket camcorder, a point-and-shoot camera that also takes movies, or an iPhone 3GS with you, that's the better camera to use.

Shooting video

To shoot video with your 5G iPod nano, just follow these steps:

1. Select Video Camera in the main screen.

2. Point the iPod at your subject, and look at the display (**Figure 3.1**).

   You can shoot in either portrait or landscape orientation.

Figure 3.1
Shooting video with the 5G iPod nano.

note The iPod will shoot in the orientation you use when you start recording. So, for example, if you hold the iPod straight up and down, you'll get a tall movie. If you rotate the iPod while shooting, the resulting video will turn on its side, just as though you were shooting with a regular camcorder.

3. Curse when you realize that your hand or finger is in the way.

The location of the nano's camera is such that when you're holding the iPod in portrait orientation, you'll cover the lens with your hand, and when you're holding it in landscape orientation, your right index finger makes an occasional appearance.

4. Hold the nano differently.

It's important to understand that you can hold the iPod in any of four directions: top pointing up, top pointing down, sideways with the click wheel on the right, and sideways with the click wheel on the left. Regardless of the direction in which you hold the iPod, the built-in accelerometer tells the iPod which way is up, so it knows its orientation and shoots video accordingly.

This means that when you're shooting in portrait orientation, you can avoid putting your hand in the way of the lens by holding the iPod upside down. If your index finger gets in the way when you shoot with the click wheel on the right, rotate the iPod 180 degrees so that the lens is on the bottom right (as you face the iPod).

tip Or don't sweat the orientation and just shoot the way people do in the nano ads: one-handed, with the click wheel on the right. Do things that way, and your fingers shouldn't obscure the lens.

5. Press and hold the Center button to choose an effect.

You can apply any of 15 effects to the video you shoot with the 5G nano: Sepia, Black & White, X-Ray, Film Grain, Thermal, Security

Cam, Cyborg, Bulge, Kaleido, Motion Blur, Mirror, Light Tunnel, Dent, Stretch, and Twirl (**Figure 3.2**). There's also a Normal setting, if you want to shoot just straight video.

Figure 3.2
Video shot with the Cyborg effect.

6. Press the Center button to record.

   Your iPod will start recording, as indicated by the small red flashing dot in the top-right corner of the display. A timer next to the recording light indicates time in hours, minutes, and seconds.

7. Press the Center button again to stop recording and save the video.

   The video frame will briefly seem to be sucked down into the display. This effect tells you that the iPod is saving the video.

8. Locate your videos.

   Click the Menu button to go to the Camera Roll screen, where you'll find clips organized by the dates when they were shot. Select an appropriate day, and press the Center button.

9. Play a video.

Videos for each day are organized on a screen that bears the date—November 14, 2009, for example. Rotate your thumb around the click wheel to select a clip, and press the Center button. The clip will fill the display and show a Play icon. Press Center again to play it.

10. Make adjustments.

The iPod nano allows you to control video playback in a variety of ways:

To Do This ...	Do This
Pause	Click the Play/Pause button.
Fast-forward through a playing video	Hold the Next button.
Rewind through a playing video	Hold the Previous button.
Move to the next video in the date screen	Click the Next button.
Move to the previous video in the date screen	Click the Previous button.
Adjust the volume	Scroll your finger around the surface of the click wheel.
Scrub the video	Click the Center button until the scroll bar appears; then scroll your finger around the surface of the click wheel.
Adjust the brightness	Click the Center button until the brightness bar appears; then scroll your finger around the surface of the click wheel to adjust brightness up or down.

Importing video

iTunes very definitely handles the lion's share of the work when it comes to synchronizing the iPod's media and data, but it adopts a strict hands-off policy when it comes to importing video from a 5G iPod nano. You must use other applications on your computer to import the nano's video. The application you use depends on whether you're using a Mac or a Windows PC.

Macintosh

With regard to importing video from the 5G iPod nano to a computer, Apple (naturally, perhaps) gives an edge to its own Macintosh. When you shoot some video with your iPod and then jack the iPod into your Mac, iTunes launches, of course—and so does iPhoto, the photo-managing and -editing application that's part of the iLife suite (which is bundled with every new Mac).

Don't let the name i*Photo* fool you. iPhoto (not i*Movie*) is indeed the application you use to import movies that you've shot with your iPod nano. To do that, just follow these steps:

1. Plug the iPod into your Mac's powered USB 2.0 port.

2. If iPhoto doesn't launch, launch it yourself.

   It's possible that you've configured the application to not launch automatically.

3. Select the iPod in iPhoto's Library pane, where it appears below the Devices heading (**Figure 3.3** on the next page).

Figure 3.3

A 5G iPod nano's videos shown in iPhoto.

4. Import your video.

    iPhoto allows you to import all the video on the iPod or just selected clips. If you'd like to import everything, simply click the Import All button at the bottom of the iPhoto window. If you'd like to import just some of the clips, hold down the Mac's Command key, click the clips you want to import to select them, and then click the Import Selected button at the bottom of the iPhoto window.

5. Locate the videos.

    Click the Last Import entry in iPhoto's Library pane, and you'll see the video clips you just imported. On your Mac, the videos will be stored here by default: *your user folder*/Pictures/iPhoto Library/Originals/ *year/date*. In this path, *your user folder* is, of course, your user folder (chris, for example) inside the Users folder at the root level of your Mac's hard drive, and *year* and *date* are the year and date when you imported (not shot) the videos.

6. Play a video.

   To play one of the videos on your Mac, just double-click it. By default, it opens and plays in Apple's QuickTime Player.

Windows

Although Apple is thrilled that Windows users also purchase iPods, it and Microsoft have made no special arrangements for an Apple application to import the movies. It's possible, however, that Windows will toss up an Autoplay window when you plug in a 5G iPod nano that contains videos. If it does, choose the option to import pictures and videos. Windows should do the right thing, pulling the videos from your iPod and storing them in your My Pictures folder (**Figure 3.4**).

Figure 3.4
iPod nano videos viewed in Windows.

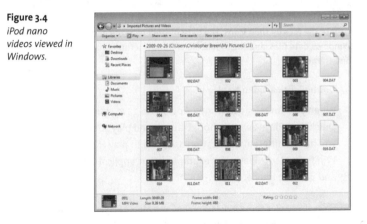

I'm being a little cagey about this situation because Windows doesn't always produce the Autoplay window. If it doesn't, try this:

1. Plug your iPod into your PC's powered USB 2.0 port.

2. Launch iTunes, if it doesn't launch automatically.

3. Select the iPod in iTunes' Source list, and in the Summary tab, enable the Enable Disk Use option.

4. Navigate to your mounted iPod.

   Click the Start menu, and locate the My Computer entry. The iPod will be listed as a removable storage device.

5. Copy the videos from the iPod to the computer.

   Double-click the iPod, and open the DCIM folder. Inside this folder, you'll see the 000APPLE folder. Inside that folder are videos marked IMG_0000, IMG_0001, IMG_0002, and so on. Select the movies, and drag them to the desktop.

note   You actually have two entries for each video—two IMG_0000 files, for example. One is a data file; the other, the movie. You can differentiate the files by their icons. The data file will bear the generic icon for all Windows data files, and the movie file will show a thumbnail of the video's first frame.

6. Double-click a video to play it.

   When you downloaded iTunes, Apple also gave your PC a copy of QuickTime Player, which should launch and play your movie. If you have a different application assigned to play H.264 videos— Windows Media Player, for example—that application will open and play the movie.

note   If you play these movies in Windows Media Player, you may see— as shown in Figure 3.4—that some movies are upside down. That's because Windows Media Player doesn't understand the orientation of these movies. QuickTime Player for Windows *does* understand, however. To view the movies in the correct orientation, use QuickTime Player or a video-playing application that allows rotation.

Radio

*Dear Reader of the Future Who Unearths This Book
from the Time Capsule Buried in My Back Yard,*

There was a time, generations before you floated across this flooded-yet-oddly-parched globe in your hoverboots, when sound came through the air. No, not as music beamed directly into your auditory cortex, but as electromagnetic waves intercepted by antennas and amplified by electronic devices called radios. *A radio could play music, commentary, news, sports broadcasts, and (increasingly) the ravings of those with a quaint social outlook.*

Years after radios had largely been eclipsed by iPods, Apple determined to throw a radio into an iPod—specifically, the 5G iPod nano. Why? Some people still enjoyed listening to radio on occasion. Others, who belonged to swanky exercise facilities, found it useful to tune their iPod's radios to the frequency on which the gym's TVs were broadcasting that day's episode of Oprah. (Oprah was like a queen of our time.) Also, I suppose, the radio was one more feature added to tempt people to purchase a new iPod.

But because Apple was Apple, this radio wasn't just any old radio. No, it was a special radio that buffered *audio—meaning that as it received radio programming, it simultaneously stored that programming in a small memory space. It stored exactly 15 minutes of audio, and when those 15 minutes elapsed, the oldest programming dripped out of that memory space to make room for new, incoming programming. You guys have found a TiVo by now, surely. Similar idea. The iPod's radio let people back up and listen to material received up to 15 minutes in the past.*

This radio received programming only on the FM band. Although the other band, AM, offered desirable content in the form of sports broadcasts, AM radios required larger circuitry than FM radios, and Apple was uninterested in fattening up its ultraslim iPod simply for the sake of a few ball games.

Hope this adds another piece to the puzzle that is the early 21st century. Sorry about the mess. If you come across any members of the Breen clan, pass along my regards.

—Chris

Operating the radio

You've got the history. Now take a look at how the 5G nano's radio works. Just follow these steps:

1. Attach the antenna.

   No, don't bother rummaging around in the iPod box. The antenna is the headset that came with the iPod. Fact is, any cable—headphone or otherwise—that you plug into the iPod's headphone port will act as an antenna. Fail to fill this port, and the iPod will tell you that the radio can't play.

2. Start the radio.

   Navigate to the Radio entry in the iPod's main screen, and click the Center button.

3. Scan available stations.

   The radio can scan stations around it that have fairly strong signals. To find one, just press and hold either Next or Previous. The radio dashes to the first robust frequency it finds and plays the station's transmission for a few seconds. If you like what you hear, click the Center button, and the iPod will stay on that station (**Figure 3.5**). Otherwise, wait a few seconds, and the radio will scan to the next strongish station.

Figure 3.5

The 5G iPod nano's radio interface.

4. Tune into a station manually.

   You don't have to scan for stations. If you know the number of a station that you want to listen to—107.5, for example—just scroll your finger around the click wheel when the tuning dial appears at the bottom of the display. The readout in the middle of the display will tick off the frequencies.

5. Save favorite stations.

   When you find a station you like, click and hold the Center button. A menu will appear at the top of the display, offering the options Add to Favorites and Cancel (**Figure 3.6** on the next page). Click Center again with Add to Favorites highlighted, and you'll save that station as a favorite. Later, you can access favorites easily by clicking the Next or Previous button; each click moves you to the next favorite in that direction. Additionally, you can call up favorites by clicking the Menu button to move to the Radio screen, selecting Favorites, clicking Center, choosing a favorite station, and clicking Center once again.

Figure 3.6
Adding a favorite radio station.

6. Turn it up (or down)!

   To adjust the radio's volume, wait for the tuning dial to disappear. (It hangs around for only about 7 seconds.) Then, at the bottom of the screen, you'll see a gray bar, which I discuss shortly. When you see that gray bar, you're welcome to adjust the iPod's volume by scrolling your finger around the click wheel.

Using the buffer

The radio's buffer is where the magic happens. If someone routinely interrupts your favorite radio programs with calls or conversations that last up to 15 minutes, you're going to love this feature.

When Lassie bursts into the room barking something about wells and small boys, for example, calmly click Play/Pause. A gray bubble will appear above the gray bar at the bottom of the radio's display. That gray bubble displays the current time (**Figure 3.7**). You've just "paused" live radio.

Figure 3.7
The radio's buffer in action.

After you've dashed to the well, extracted the kid, cautioned him that falling into four wells in a week is a bit much, and returned to your iPod, press Play/Pause again. The radio broadcast will pick up exactly where you left off, because the programming that played during your absence has been stored in the iPod's memory.

But suppose that in all the excitement, you lost the thread of what was being talked about during the broadcast. No problem. Click Play/Pause again, and when you see the gray time bubble, scroll your finger counterclockwise around the click wheel to "rewind" the broadcast. The time bubble will move to the left, and the time will decrease. When you find a spot that makes sense, stop scrolling, and press Play/Pause to play the buffered broadcast from that point.

The buffer is completely temporary. You can't record radio in the sense that you can save it and then transfer it to your computer via iTunes. When those 15 minutes have elapsed, the buffer stops, and whatever played 15 minutes and 1 second ago is gone.

note When you change stations, the buffer is cleared. If you hope to rewind in time, don't station-surf.

iTunes Tagging

The iPod's radio has one additional noteworthy feature: iTunes Tagging. This feature takes advantage of the fact that some radio stations' signals contain embedded information. This information, which is displayed on compatible radios, can include the station's call letters, program title, and track and artist names. The track and artist names are our concern here.

When track and artist information appears below a station's frequency number on your 5G iPod nano, along with a small tag icon, you've tuned into a station that supports iTunes Tagging. This information can be saved to your iPod and, when you sync that iPod to your computer, transferred to your Mac or Windows PC.

Who cares? You, perhaps. Suppose that you're listening to a station and hear a terrific song. This station is lax about telling you the name of songs, and before you know it, it's off to commercial, leaving you wondering. If that station offers iTunes Tagging, you can save that song's title and artist to your iPod by doing this:

1. Hold down the Center button.

   When a station that supports iTunes Tagging is tuned in and a song is playing (you can't tag commercials, news, or DJ chatter, naturally), holding down the Center button produces a drop-down menu that includes the Tag command, along with Add to Favorites and Cancel (**Figure 3.8**).

Figure 3.8
Tagging a radio station.

2. Choose Tag, and click the Center button.

   The song is tagged and added to the Tagged Songs screen (**Figure 3.9**), which you access by clicking the Menu button, choosing Tagged Songs in the resulting Radio screen, and clicking the Center button.

Figure 3.9
The Tagged Songs screen.

Tagged Songs
Back In The Saddle Aerosmith
Bargain Who
Eminence Front Who
Under Pleasure P
Sunset Grill Don Henley
Ego Beyonce
Best I Ever Had Drake

 The iPod also keeps track of recently played songs on stations that support iTunes Tagging. You'll find these tracks by clicking the Recent Songs entry in the Radio screen.

3. Sync your iPod, and marvel.

When you next sync your iPod with iTunes, a green Tagged entry will appear below the Store heading in iTunes' Source list. Select this entry, and you'll see a list of all the tracks you've tagged on your iPod (**Figure 3.10**). This list contains the track name and artist, and sometimes the album.

Purchased on Upstairs …	◢	Name	Artist	Album	Price	Genre	Time
Tagged	1	☑ Best I Ever Had	Drake		VIEW		
	2	☑ Ego	Beyonce		VIEW		
▼ DEVICES	3	☑ Sunset Grill	Don Henley	Building the Perfect Beast	$0.99 BUY SONG	Rock	6:19
▶ 16GB 5G nano	4	☑ Under	Pleasure P		VIEW		
▶ SHARED	5	☑ Eminence Front	The Who	The Who: The Ultimate Collection	$0.99 BUY SONG	Rock	5:37
	6	☑ Broken	I-94	Control	$0.99 BUY SONG	Alternative	4:28
▼ GENIUS	7	☑ Back in the Saddle (Live)	Aerosmith	A Little South of Sanity (Live)	$0.99 BUY SONG	Rock	5:56

Figure 3.10 *Tagged songs listed in iTunes.*

4. View or buy a tagged track.

Within the Price column, you'll see either a View or Buy Song button along with the price of the track. Click View, and (provided that you have a live Internet connection) you're taken to the iTunes Store, where you'll see the track either as a single or as part of an album. Click Buy Song, and you'll be prompted for your Apple ID and password so that you can purchase the track without having to visit the Store (which I cover in Chapter 5).

Pedometer

The 5G iPod nano can keep track of your steps with its built-in pedometer and accelerometer. When the accelerometer detects the kind of bump associated with a footfall, its counter increases by 1. This feature is unlike the Nike + iPod Sports Kit—a hardware/software package for earlier iPods that measures and records the length and frequency of your stride and then manages and records a workout based on that data. The nano's pedometer simply counts steps; it cares not a whit how quickly you took those steps or whether you took them on the flat or while trudging up a mountain.

Viewing the Fitness screen

The Fitness screen is the gateway to the pedometer, its settings, and the history of your workout (or walkouts, if you prefer a gentler form of exercise). It shakes out this way.

Pedometer

To use the pedometer, select Extras in the Main menu, click Center, select Fitness, and click Center again. In the Fitness screen that appears, select Pedometer, and click Center one more time.

You'll see the Choose Weight screen first. Just scroll your finger around the click wheel until you arrive at your weight, and press the Center button. (And hey, if you want to shave a few pounds off that estimate, that's completely between you and your iPod.) You'll go to the Steps screen (**Figure 3.11**), which—not surprisingly—is where you see the number of steps you've taken, along with a small calorie counter and a timer that tracks the time since you started the pedometer.

Figure 3.11
The pedometer's
Steps screen.

note   **Obviously, the calorie counter is making the roughest guess at how quickly you're burning energy. Best to think of it as being a motivational tool.**

To stop your workout, just click the Center button. In the Fitness screen that appears, you can return to the Pedometer screen by selecting Pedometer and clicking Center.

Settings

The Settings command in the Fitness screen generates four options:

▪ **Pedometer**

   You can choose whether the pedometer will run at all times or only when you invoke it.

▪ **Daily Step Goal**

   When you choose this option and click the Center button, you find a variety of options, ranging from None to 2,500 to 25,000 to 100,000 (and some settings in between). You also have the option to enter a custom setting and enter steps in increments of 1,000 until you reach 10,000. At that point, increments are in tens of thousands (10,000, 20,000, and so on).

   Your step goal appears on the pedometer's History screen, along with the number of steps you actually took on a given day.

▪ **Weight**

   If your weight has changed, you're welcome to likewise change it on your iPod by invoking this command and entering a new value.

▪ **Screen orientation**

   A lot of people will want to watch the pedometer's readout as they exercise. Displaying that readout in a vertical view may not be convenient, depending on the way you've strapped on your iPod. Fortunately,

this command lets you view the pedometer in right or left landscape
orientation.

History

This final command gives you an idea of how you've been doing. Invoke
the History command, and you see a calendar screen that displays the
current month. Those days when you've switched on the pedometer have
a small dot below the date. Using the click wheel, select a day that has
one of these dots, and click the Center button.

The resulting Session History screen indicates the total number of steps
recorded that day, along with the date (**Figure 3.12**). Below that display is
a list that includes this data: Step Goal, Duration, Start Time, End Time,
Calories, For the Week, and Month Total.

Figure 3.12
*The pedometer's
Session History
screen.*

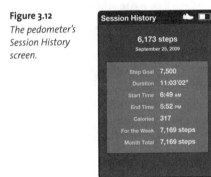

Turn the iPod to landscape orientation, and you see this data marked out
on a graph. Even if you have the pedometer configured so that it's always
on, the information in the History screen and graph won't update as you
walk. Return to the pedometer screen, however, and you'll see that the
iPod has continued to record your steps.

Syncing with Nike+ Active

As much fun as it is to look at this data on your iPod, it's more fun to track it on your computer, and Apple and Nike have made it possible to do just that. All you need are your 5G iPod nano and a free Nike+ Active account. The process works like this:

1. Plug your iPod into your computer.

   If your nano has pedometer data on it, iTunes pops up a dialog box asking whether you'd like to transfer your workout data to iTunes and view it on the Nike+ Active Web site.

2. Sign up for a Nike+ Active account.

   If this sounds like fun to you, click the Learn More button in the dialog box. Your Web browser will open and take you to Nike's Web site. Click the Join button on this site, and you'll be walked through the process for signing up for a free Nike+ account.

3. Send your steps to Nike.

   After you've established an account, you can send your step data to Nike. You do this simply by clicking the Send button in the dialog box that iTunes displays whenever your iPod has new pedometer data.

   If you click Send, another dialog box asks whether you'd like to visit the site (**Figure 3.13**). Click Don't Visit if you'd rather not or Visit if you'd like to pay a call.

Figure 3.13

Why not pay Nike's Web site a visit?

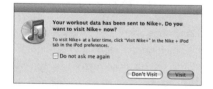

tip You can visit the Nike site at any time by selecting your iPod nano in iTunes' Source list, clicking the Nike + iPod tab that appears in the main window, and then clicking the Visit Nike+ button.

4. View your progress.

When you visit the site and log in, you'll see your progress laid out in several views, the first of which is a skyscraper (**Figure 3.14**). If you record 4,500 steps, you've climbed the equivalent of a 100-story skyscraper. When you've achieved that goal, you can move on to other goals (stepping enough to work off the caloric content of a hot dog or doughnut, for example).

Figure 3.14
Track your pedometer progress on Nike's Web site.

At the bottom of the page, you'll see the number of steps you've recorded and synced each day that week, your best day's total number of steps, the total number of steps you've recorded and synced for the week, and all the steps you've ever recorded and synced. Again, this feature isn't hard science, but a fun motivational tool.

Voice Memos

Although voice memos aren't completely new to the iPod nano, the 5G model is the first nano that doesn't require an external microphone to record them, thanks to the small microphone that sits above the video-camera lens on the back of the iPod.

To record a voice memo, follow these steps:

1. Launch Voice Memos.

   To do this, select Extras in the iPod's main screen, click the Center button, scroll down to Voice Memos, and click Center again. The resulting screen displays a microphone similar to the one you'd see in the Voice Memos app on an iPhone (**Figure 3.15**).

Figure 3.15
The 5G iPod nano's Voice Memos screen.

2. Record a memo.

   Click the Center button, and the iPod starts recording. While it records, you see a red Recording bar and a time readout at the top of the display. The needle on the VU meter responds to the sound coming into the microphone, registering greater movement for louder sounds.

tip **Even though the microphone is on the back of the iPod, you needn't flip it around for the iPod to hear you. The microphone manages to record sound coming from the front quite well. You'll get a better tone from the microphone if you indeed speak into it, however.**

3. Insert a chapter mark.

To insert a chapter mark into your recording, click Center. The iPod will continue to record. Later, when you copy the voice memos to iTunes (see step 7), you can select the voice memo in iTunes and then select a chapter to listen to by choosing it from the Chapters menu in iTunes' menu bar.

4. Save your recording.

When you click the Play/Pause button, a menu appears that includes Resume, Delete, and Stop and Save options. Choose Stop and Save to save your recording.

5. Locate your memos.

When you chose Stop and Save, you were taken to the Voice Memos screen, which displays New Memo and Voice Memos commands. Choose Voice Memos, and click the Center button. In the resulting Voice Memos screen, you'll see any voice memos that you've recorded since you last synced your iPod. Choose one, and click the Center button.

6. Play, label, or delete your memo.

In the data screen that you now see, you have the option to play, label, or delete the memo. Choose Play and click the Center button, and you'll hear the memo played through the iPod's speakers or the audio device plugged into the headphone port or Dock connector.

If you choose Label and click Center, you have the option to label your memo as a podcast, interview, lecture, idea, meeting, or memo.

Delete, of course, vaporizes the memo.

7. Sync your memos to your computer.

When you next sync your iPod to your computer, its voice memos are copied to your iTunes Library automatically, titled with the date and time when they were recorded—*10/31/09 11:35 AM*, for example. These files are recorded in AAC format at 128 Kbps (see Chapter 4 for information about formats and bit rates).

4

iTunes and You

A high-performance automobile is little more than an interesting amalgam of metal and plastic if it's missing tires and fuel. Sure, given the proper slope (and, perhaps, a helpful tailwind), that car is capable of movement, but the resulting journey leaves much to be desired. So, too, the iPod is a less-capable music-making vehicle without Apple's multitrick media manager/player, iTunes. The two—like coffee and cream, dill and pickle, Fred and Ginger—were simply meant for each other.

To best understand what makes the iPod's world turn, you must be familiar with how it and iTunes 9 work together to move music (as well as pictures, videos, and games, in the case of some recent iPods) on and off your iPod. In the following pages, you'll see just that.

Getting the Goods

"Eep!" I hear you squeep. "I've never used iTunes or owned an iPod. I have no idea how to get music into iTunes, much less put it on my portable music player. What do I do?"

Relax. I'm not going to tell you how to put your music and movies on your iPod classic or nano until you know how to assemble a music and movie library.

I'll start with music. You have three ways to get tunes into iTunes:

- Recording (or *ripping*, in today's terminology) an audio CD

- Importing music that doesn't come directly from a CD (such as an audio track you downloaded or created in an audio application on your computer)

- Purchasing music from an online emporium such as Apple's iTunes Store

The following sections tell you how to use the first two methods. The iTunes Store is a special-enough place that I devote all of Chapter 5 to it.

> **note** The procedures for adding movies and videos are similar, except that iTunes offers no option for ripping DVDs. You can do that, but the procedure is more complicated than ripping an audio CD. I cover ripping DVDs in Chapter 8.

Rip a CD

Apple intended the process of converting audio-CD music to computer data to be painless, and it is. Here's how to go about it:

1. Launch iTunes.

2. Insert an audio CD into your computer's CD or DVD drive.

By default, iTunes tries to identify the CD you've inserted. It logs on to the Web to download the CD's track information—a very handy feature for those who find typing such minutia to be tedious.

The CD appears in iTunes' Source list under the Devices heading, and the track info appears in the Song list to the right (**Figure 4.1**).

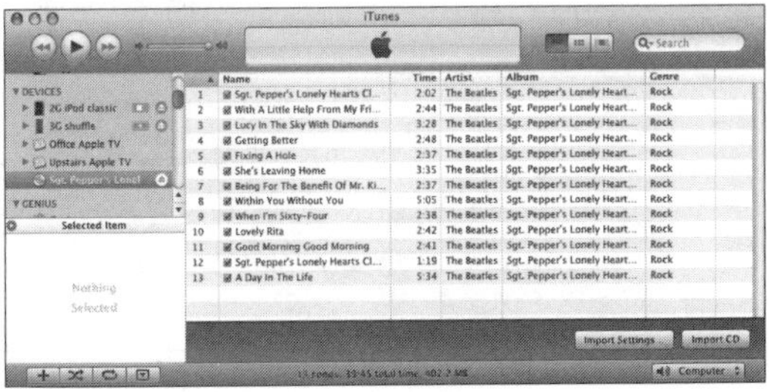

Figure 4.1
A selected CD and its tracks.

Then iTunes displays a dialog box, asking whether you'd like to import the tracks from the CD into your iTunes Library.

3. Click Yes, and iTunes imports the songs; click No, and it doesn't.

note You can change this behavior in iTunes' Preferences window. In the General preference, you find a When You Insert a CD pop-up menu. Make a choice from that menu to direct iTunes to show the CD, begin playing it, ask to import it (the default), import it without asking, or import and then eject it.

4. If you decided earlier not to import the audio but want to do so now, simply select the CD in the Source list and click the Import CD button in the bottom-right section of the iTunes window.

iTunes begins encoding the files via the method chosen in the Import Settings window (**Figure 4.2** on the next page), which you access by opening iTunes' Preferences window (choose iTunes > Preferences on a Mac or Edit > Preferences on a Windows PC), clicking the General tab, and clicking the Import Settings button. By default, iTunes imports songs in iTunes Plus AAC format at 256 Kbps. (For more on encoding methods, see the sidebar "Import Business: File Formats and Bit Rates" in the next section.)

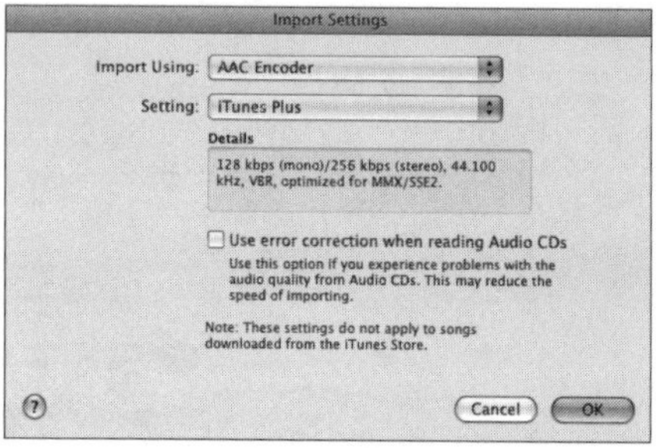

Figure 4.2

iTunes' Import Settings window.

Import Settings

Import Using: AAC Encoder

Setting: iTunes Plus

Details

128 kbps (mono)/256 kbps (stereo), 44.100 kHz, VBR, optimized for MMX/SSE2.

☐ Use error correction when reading Audio CDs

Use this option if you experience problems with the audio quality from Audio CDs. This may reduce the speed of importing.

Note: These settings do not apply to songs downloaded from the iTunes Store.

Cancel   OK

tip To import only certain songs, uncheck the boxes next to the titles of songs you don't want to import; then click the Import CD button.

Combining CD Tracks

There may be occasions when you don't want iTunes to extract individual tracks from a CD, such as when you have a long audiobook that's stored on multiple CDs, and each CD has a dozen or more individual files that represent portions of chapters. Managing what may turn out to be dozens of chapters on an iPod is anything but convenient. To work around a problem like this one, you can combine all the tracks on the CD into a single long track.

To do that, insert the CD, turn down iTunes' offer to rip the CD for you, select the CD in iTunes' Source list, select all the tracks on the CD, and choose Advanced > Join CD Tracks. The contents of the CD will be ripped as one long file.

5. Click the Music entry in the Source list.

You'll find the songs you just imported somewhere in the list.

6. To listen to a song, click its name in the list and then click the Play icon or press the spacebar.

Move music into iTunes

Ripping CDs isn't the only way to put music files on your computer. Suppose that you've downloaded some audio files from the Web and want to put them in iTunes. You have three ways to do that:

- In iTunes, choose File > Add to Library.

   When you choose this command, the Add To Library dialog box appears (**Figure 4.3**). Navigate to the file, folder, or volume you want to add to iTunes, and click Open. iTunes determines which files it thinks it can play and adds them to the library.

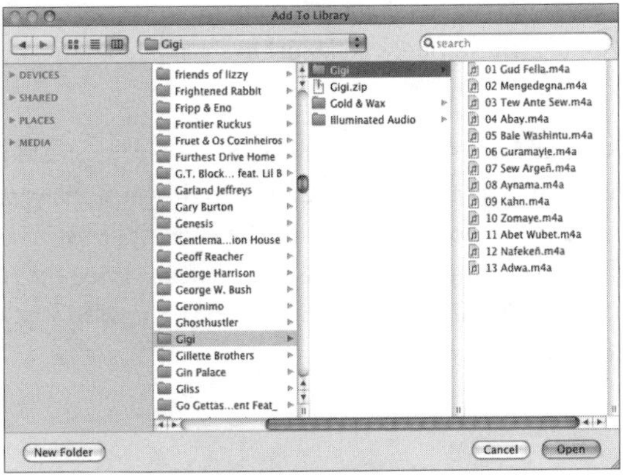

Figure 4.3

Navigate to tracks you want to add to iTunes via the Add To Library dialog box.

- Drag files, folders, or entire volumes to the iTunes icon in Mac OS X's Dock, the iTunes icon in Windows' Start menu (if you've pinned iTunes to this menu), or the iTunes icon in either operating system (at which point iTunes launches and adds the dragged files to its library).

- Drag files, folders, or entire volumes into iTunes' main window or the Library entry in the Source list.

  In the Mac versions of iTunes, by default you'll find songs in the iTunes Music folder within the iTunes folder inside the Music folder inside your Mac OS X user folder. The path to my iTunes music files, for example, would be chris/Music/iTunes/iTunes Music.

  Windows users will find their iTunes Music folder by following this path: *yourusername*/My Music (XP) or Music (Vista and Windows 7)/iTunes/iTunes Music.

You can use the same methods to add compatible videos and movies to your iTunes Library. (For more on what makes those videos compatible, see the sidebar "Working with Supported Video Formats" later in the chapter.) Those videos will most likely appear in the Movies playlist in the Source list.

I say *most likely* because there are a few exceptions: Videos specifically designated as music videos appear in the Music playlist, videos designated as TV shows appear in the TV Shows playlist, and video podcasts are filed under Podcasts in iTunes' Source list. See the sidebar "Tag, You're It" later in this chapter for information on how to apply those video designations.

Import Business:
File Formats and Bit Rates

MP3, MPEG-4, AAC, AIFF, WAV . . . is the computer industry incapable of speaking plain English?

It may seem so, given the plethora of acronyms floating through modern-day Technotopia. But the lingo and the basics behind it aren't terribly difficult to understand.

MP3, AAC, AIFF, and WAV are audio file formats. The compression methods used to create MP3 and AAC files are termed *lossy* because their encoders remove information from the source sound file to create these smaller files. Fortunately, these encoders are designed to remove the information you're least likely to miss—audio frequencies that humans can't hear easily, for example.

AIFF and WAV files are uncompressed, which means that they contain all the data in the source audio file. When a Macintosh pulls audio from an audio CD, it does so in AIFF format, which is the native uncompressed audio format used by Apple's QuickTime technology. WAV is an AIFF variant used extensively with the Windows operating system.

iTunes supports one other compression format: Apple Lossless. This format is termed a *lossless* encoder because it shrinks files by removing redundant data without discarding any portion of the audio spectrum. This scheme yields sound files with all the audio quality of the source files at around half their size. iTunes and the iPod also support the H.264 and MPEG-4 video formats. These, too, are compressed formats that allow you to fit a great big movie on a tiny iPod.

Now that you're familiar with these file formats, I'll touch on resolution as it applies to audio and video files.

(continued on next page)

Import Business:
File Formats and Bit Rates (continued)

You probably know that the more pixels per inch a digital photo-graph has, the crisper the image (and the larger the file). Resolution applies to audio as well. But audio defines resolution by the number of kilobits per second (Kbps) contained in an audio file. *With files encoded similarly,* the higher the kilobit rate, the better-sounding the file (and the larger the file).

I emphasize *with files encoded similarly* because the quality of the file depends a great deal on the encoder used to compress it. Many people claim that if you encode a file at 128 Kbps in both the MP3 and AAC formats, the AAC file sounds better.

The Import Settings menu (which you reach by clicking the Import Settings button within iTunes' General preferences) lets you choose to import files in AAC, AIFF, Apple Lossless, MP3, or WAV format. The Setting pop-up menu is where you choose the resolution of the AAC and MP3 files encoded by iTunes by choosing Custom from the menu. iTunes' default setting is iTunes Plus (256 Kbps). To change this setting, choose High Quality (128 Kbps) or Custom from the Setting pop-up menu. (Spoken Podcast is another option when you choose the AAC Encoder, but it pro-duces quality that's good only for spoken-word audio.) If you choose Custom, the AAC Encoder dialog box appears. Choose a different setting—16 Kbps to 320 Kbps—from the Stereo Bit Rate pop-up menu (**Figure 4.4**). Files encoded at a high bit rate sound better than those encoded at a low bit rate (such as 96 Kbps).

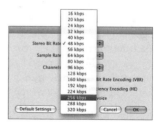

Figure 4.4 *The Stereo Bit Rate pop-up menu.*

Import Business:
File Formats and Bit Rates (continued)

But files encoded at higher bit rates also take up more space on your hard drive and iPod.

The preset options for MP3 importing include Good Quality (128 Kbps), High Quality (160 Kbps), and Higher Quality (192 Kbps). If you don't care to use one of these settings, choose Custom from this same pop-up menu. In the MP3 Encoder dialog box that appears, you have the option to choose a bit rate ranging from 16 Kbps to 320 Kbps.

Resolution is important for video as well. Fortunately (because an explanation beyond this gross simplification is beyond the scope of this slim volume), iTunes allows you to convert video to only two formats: iPod/iPhone–compatible format and Apple TV format. You do this by choosing Advanced > Create iPod or iPhone Version or Create Apple TV Version, respectively. These commands provide no tools for adjusting resolution settings.

Creating and Configuring a Playlist

Before you put any media files (music or video) on your iPod, organize them in iTunes. Doing so will make it far easier to find the media you want, both on your computer and on your iPod. The best way to organize that material is through playlists.

A *playlist* is simply a set of tracks and/or videos that you believe should be grouped in a list. The organizing principle is completely up to you. You can organize songs by artist, by mood, by style, by song length . . . heck, if you like, you can have iTunes automatically gather all your 1950s polka tunes with the letter *z* in their titles. Similarly, you can organize your videos by criteria including director, actor, and TV-series title. You can mix videos and music tracks within playlists as well, combining, say, music videos and music tracks by the same artist. As far as playlists are concerned, you're the boss.

The following sections look at ways to create playlists.

Standard playlists

Standard playlists are those that you make by hand, selecting each of the media files you want grouped. To create a standard playlist in iTunes, follow these steps:

1. Click the large plus (+) icon in the bottom-left corner of the iTunes window, or choose File > New Playlist (Command-N on the Mac, Ctrl+N in Windows).

2. In the highlighted field that appears next to that new playlist in the Source list, type a name for your new playlist.

3. Click an appropriate entry in the Source list—Music, Movies, TV Shows, or Podcasts—and select the tracks or videos you want to place in the playlist you created.

4. Drag the selected tracks or videos to the new playlist's icon.

5. Arrange the order of the tracks or videos in your new playlist.

   To do this, click the Number column in the main window, and drag tracks up and down in the list. When the iPod is synchronized with iTunes, this order is how the songs will appear in the playlist on your iPod.

   If the songs in your playlist come from the same album, and you want the songs in the playlist to appear in the same order as they do on the original album, click the Album heading.

Playlist from selection

You can also create a new playlist from selected items by following these steps:

1. Command-click (Mac) or Ctrl+click (Windows) songs or videos to select the files you'd like to appear in the new playlist.

2. Choose File > New Playlist from Selection (Command-Shift-N on a Mac, Ctrl+Shift+N on a Windows PC).

   A new playlist containing the selected items will appear under the Playlists heading in the iTunes Source list. If all selected tracks are from the same album, the list will bear the name of the artist and album. If the tracks are from different albums by the same artist, the playlist will be named after the artist. If you've mixed tracks from different artists or combined music with videos, the new playlist will display the name *untitled playlist*.

3. To name (or rename) the playlist, type in the highlighted field.

Smart Playlists

Smart Playlists are slightly different beasts. They include tracks that meet certain conditions you've defined—for example, Fountains of Wayne tracks encoded in AAC format that are shorter than 4 minutes. Here's how to work the magic of a basic Smart Playlist:

1. In iTunes, choose File > New Smart Playlist (Command-Option-N on the Mac, Ctrl+Alt+N in Windows).

   You can also hold down the Option key on the Mac or the Shift key on a Windows PC and then click the gear icon that replaces the plus icon at the bottom of the iTunes window.

2. Choose your criteria.

You'll spy a pop-up menu that allows you to select items by various
criteria—including artist, composer, genre, podcast, bit rate, comment,
date added, and last played—followed by a Contains field. To choose
all songs by Elvis Presley and Elvis Costello, for example, you'd choose
Artist from the pop-up menu and then enter **Elvis** in the Contains
field (**Figure 4.5**).

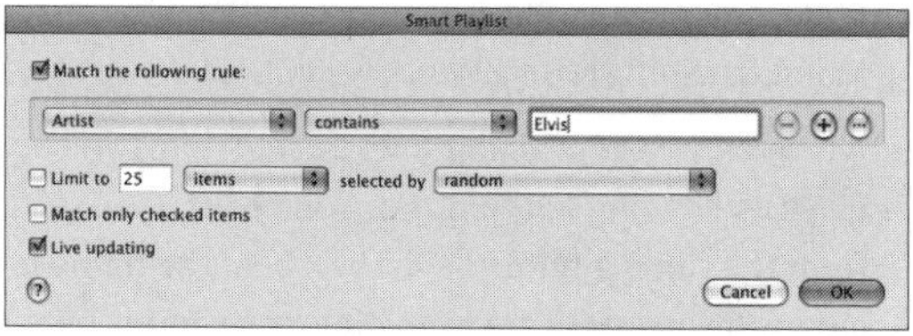

Figure 4.5
*The inner
workings of a
simple Smart
Playlist.*

You can limit the selections that appear in the playlist by minutes,
hours, megabytes, gigabytes, or number of songs. You may want the
playlist to contain no more than 2 GB worth of songs and videos, for
example.

You'll also see a Live Updating option. When it's switched on, this
option ensures that if you add to iTunes any songs or videos that
meet the criteria you've set, those files will be added to the playlist.
If you add a new Elvis Costello album to iTunes, for example, iTunes
updates your Elvis Smart Playlist automatically.

3. Click OK.

   A new playlist that contains your smart selections appears in iTunes'
   Source list.

You don't have to settle for a single criterion. By clicking the plus icon
next to a criterion field, you can add other conditions. You could create
a playlist containing, say, only songs you've never listened to by punk
artists whose names contain the letter *J*.

Conditional Smart Playlists

With iTunes 9, you can create more powerful Smart Playlists than you could before, thanks to a new feature called *nested conditional rules*. With nested conditional rules, you have sets and subsets of rules that can act on previous rules. Perhaps you want a Smart Playlist that picks out music and music-video files that are less than 4 minutes long, that were recorded before 1990, and that fall within the Pop and Soul genres. It would be difficult to get this level of detail in a traditional Smart Playlist—but not quite so difficult in a Smart Playlist that contains nested conditional rules. **Figure 4.6** shows settings for an example conditional Smart Playlist.

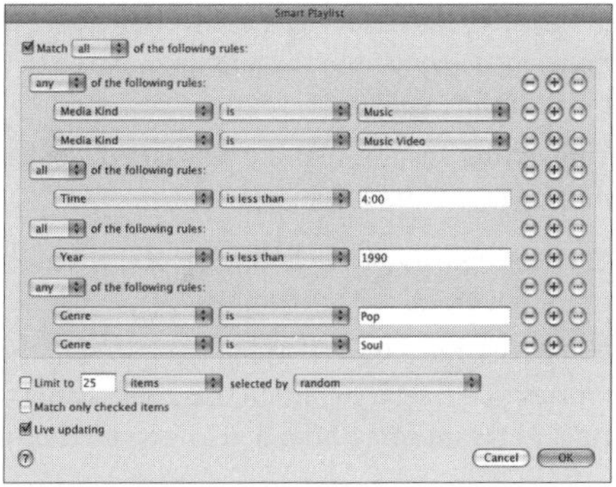

Figure 4.6

A conditional Smart Playlist.

A good way to see how to use nested conditional rules is to duplicate the settings in Figure 4.6. (Later, you can follow this same procedure but choose different settings for your own conditional Smart Playlists.) Follow these steps:

1. In iTunes, choose File > New Smart Playlist (Command-Option-N on the Mac, Ctrl-Alt-N in Windows).

(continued on next page)

Conditional Smart Playlists (continued)

2. In the resulting Smart Playlist window, click the ellipsis (...) button to expand the window.

3. Click the minus (–) button to remove the top condition, which reads (above the pop-up menu) *Artist Contains*.

   For nesting to work properly, you need to start with a conditional, and that first default entry prevents you from doing that.

4. Click the plus (+) button next to *Artist Contains* to create another condition. Configure the two conditions to read *Media Kind is Music* and *Media Kind is Music Video*.

5. In the *All of the Following Rules* section above these two conditions, choose *Any* from the pop-up menu so that it reads *Any of the Following Rules*.

   This setting ensures that the playlist will look for both music and music-video files.

6. Click the ellipsis button at the top of the window to add another condition group.

   If you click the ellipsis button next to one of the Media Kind entries, you'll set a condition that affects only that Media Kind rule. You want something that affects all chosen files.

7. In the new condition group, create a rule that reads *Time is Less Than 4:00*.

   That takes care of the time limit.

8. Click the top ellipsis button again, and create a rule that reads *Year is Less Than 1990*.

   So much for the date.

9. Click the top ellipsis button just one more time to create one last group.

Conditional Smart Playlists (continued)

10. In this group, add two genre conditions that read *Genre is Pop* and *Genre is Soul*.

11. Above these Genre entries, change *All of the Following Rules* to *Any of the Following Rules*.

    Changing *All* to *Any* instructs the playlist to look for any tracks that meet the previous conditions and that are tagged with any of these two genres.

Folders for playlists

You can also file playlists in folders. By invoking the File > New Playlist Folder command, you can lump a bunch of playlists into a single folder. Folders are a great way to keep your playlists separate from your spouse's or to gather groups of similar playlists (All My Jazz Playlists, for example).

At one time, folders didn't translate to the iPod; however, the 3G–5G iPod nanos and the iPod classics do offer nested playlist hierarchies.

Genius playlists and mixes

If you're the kind of reader who starts at the beginning of a book and plows through to the end, you're already aware (from Chapter 2) of the Genius feature on the iPod. iTunes 9 can also create Genius playlists, as well as Genius Mixes (which I also touch on in Chapter 2). As a reminder, Genius playlists are collections of music that iTunes believes to be related to other music in your library, and Genius Mixes are 250-track playlists chosen by genre from your iTunes Library. In the following sections, I look at the ins and outs of each feature.

Genius playlists

To create Genius playlists with iTunes, follow these steps:

1. Switch on the Genius feature.

   When you install iTunes, you're offered the choice to turn Genius on. Doing so requires an iTunes account. If you don't have one, no worries; when you start the Genius process, you'll find an option for signing up for an account. If you neglected to turn on Genius, you can do so by choosing Store > Turn on Genius. If you're connected to the Internet, iTunes will ask you to sign into your iTunes account.

2. Wait while iTunes configures Genius.

   iTunes gathers information about your music library—specifically, the songs it contains—and sends that information to Apple's servers anonymously. That information is compared with similar data from other users and placed in a database. A database file that contains the relationship data is sent back to your computer.

3. Create a Genius playlist.

   Select a track in your iTunes Library, and click the Genius button in the bottom-right corner of the iTunes window. iTunes will create a new playlist of 25 songs (by default) that should go well with the track you selected. You can ask Genius to create a longer version of this playlist by making a larger choice from the Limit To pop-up menu at the bottom of the window; your choices are 25, 50, 75, and 100 songs. You can also click Refresh to ask Genius to try again.

4. Save the playlist.

   When you click the Save Playlist button at the top of the window, iTunes creates a playlist named after your source track—*A Common Disaster*, for example. You can return to any Genius playlist you've created and change the Limit To settings as well as refresh the playlist.

5. Expose the Genius sidebar.

Click the Sidebar icon in the bottom-right corner of the iTunes window to display the Genius sidebar, which is designed to recommend related music from the iTunes Store (**Figure 4.7**).

At the top of the sidebar, you'll find entries that include the name of the artist, Also by This Artist (which includes Top Albums and Top Songs entries), and Genius Recommendations. You might also see an iTunes Essentials entry. A small arrow icon next to an entry indicates a trip to the iTunes Store. Click an artist's name, for example, and you'll be taken to the Store page devoted to that artist. Click the arrow icon next to Genius Recommendations, and iTunes creates a list of those recommendations. (Though this list looks like a playlist, you can't save it as such.)

Figure 4.7
The Genius sidebar.

Next to the song selections, you'll see both a Preview button (denoted by a small Play icon) and a Buy button. To audition 30 seconds of a track, just click the Preview button. If you like what you've heard and would like to own the track, click Buy. In the resulting dialog box, you'll be prompted for your Apple ID and password. Enter that info and click the Buy button, and the track downloads to your computer.

> **note**   You can sync Genius playlists to your iPod just as you can any other playlists.

Genius Mixes

Genius Mixes are new in iTunes 9 and, as I write this chapter, supported only by the 5G iPod nano, 2G iPod touch, and iPhone. Genius Mixes are broader tools than Genius playlists in that they're created based on genres—Rock, Jazz, and Classical, for example.

The "genius" of Genius Mixes is that their content is still related, much as is content for a Genius playlist. Unless you have a small music library, it's unlikely that iTunes will produce a Genius Mix including AC/DC, Donovan, Sheryl Crow, and Ry Cooder, even though all four artists may have had a Rock genre tag applied to them. Instead, you may have one Rock Genius mix that includes '60s artists such as Janis Joplin, Cream, Jimi Hendrix, and The Small Faces. Another Genius Mix could include modern pop artists such as Death Cab for Cutie, The Finn Brothers, The Apples in Stereo, and Feist. So thanks to the enormous database of related music first created when the Genius feature was introduced with iTunes 8, iTunes has the power to create these large mixes that make sense.

Creating them is really easy:

1. Launch iTunes 9 or later.

2. Click the Genius Mixes entry located under the Genius heading in iTunes' Source list.

3. There is no step 3.

iTunes will create up to 12 Genius Mixes. Each Genius Mix is represented by an album cover that, in turn, features four album covers taken from the music in that Genius Mix (**Figure 4.8**). An example Rock Genius Mix, then, could include album artwork from Coldplay, Radiohead, Oasis, and John Mayer albums.

Figure 4.8
Genius Mixes.

Unlike Genius playlists, Genius Mixes can't be edited. In fact, you can't even see the contents of one of these mixes. What iTunes provides is exactly what you get. To play one, just click its icon, and the first track in the mix plays. To skip to the next track, click the Next button in iTunes' play controls (located in the top-left corner of the iTunes window) or press your keyboard's right-arrow key.

As I said, Genius Mixes can be synced only to the 5G iPod nano, the iPod touch, and the iPhone (iPod touch and iPhone 3.1 software required). To sync Genius Mixes, do this:

1. Select your compatible device in iTunes' Source list.

2. Click the Music tab.

3. Enable the Sync Music option.

4. Enable the Selected Playlists, Artists, and Genres option.

5. In the Playlists column, look for the Genius Mixes entry; then select all of these mixes (by checking the Genius Mixes check box) or specific mixes (**Figure 4.9**).

Figure 4.9

Selecting Genius Mixes to sync to a 5G iPod nano.

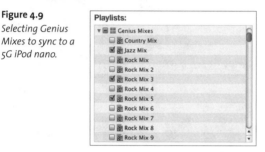

6. Sync the device.

 If you choose to sync all your music with the iPod, Genius Mixes will be included automatically. If you don't have enough room on the iPod to sync your entire music library, however, Genius Mixes won't be added— which makes sense, as each Genius Mix includes 250 tracks.

As I point out in Chapter 2, on the 5G iPod nano, you find the Genius Mixes command in the Music screen. Select it, and the first Genius Mix appears on the iPod's screen—again, represented by four album covers. To play the Genius Mix, click the Play/Pause button. To skip to the next song in the mix, click the Next button. To skip back a track, click the Previous button twice (clicking once takes you to the beginning of the currently playing track).

 To move to another Genius Mix (if you have more than one on your iPod, of course), stop playback and click the Next button.

Configuring iTunes

Intuitive though it may be, iTunes packs a lot of features and power—
enough that I could write an entire book about just this application.
I have bigger fish to fry: showing you how to get the most out of your
iPod. But part of frying those fish is introducing the key iTunes features
that can make using and listening to your iPod more enjoyable. In this
section, I examine those features.

Setting iTunes preferences

Choose iTunes > Preferences on a Mac or Edit > Preferences on a Windows
PC, and you open iTunes' Preferences window. Some of the tabs within
this window lead to settings that you should know about.

General

I've already mentioned that within the General preference, you specify
what happens when you insert a CD. Elsewhere in this tab, you find
options for showing or hiding certain items in iTunes' Source list, including Movies, TV Shows, Podcasts, iTunes U, Audiobooks, Applications,
Ringtones, Radio, iTunes DJ, and Genius. If you find iTunes' interface too
cluttered, disabling the items you don't use will clean things up.

One of iTunes' most important features is hidden behind the Import
Settings button in the General preference. Click Import Settings to open
the window of the same name, and you find iTunes' encoder settings—
the settings you configure to determine which codec iTunes uses to rip
CDs and convert audio files, as well as what bit rates the encoder uses.
I explain the workings of encoders and bit rates earlier in this chapter,
in the "Import Business: File Formats and Bit Rates" sidebar.

tip The Import Settings window also includes the Use Error Correction When Reading Audio CDs option. If you're having difficulty ripping an audio CD (because it's dirty, for example), enable this option. iTunes will try that much harder to rip the CD properly, though the process will take longer.

Playback

Here, you can determine where in the iTunes interface movies, TV shows, and music videos are displayed (in a separate window, for example) and set the default and subtitle languages for movies. It's also within this preference that you instruct iTunes to play videos in standard definition by default and show closed captions when they're available. But the most interesting settings here are Crossfade Songs, Sound Enhancer, and Sound Check:

- **Crossfade Songs.** This setting causes the end of each song to fade out and the beginning of the next track to fade in. For some people, this feature makes for a less jarring listening experience. You can set the length of the crossfade—1 to 12 seconds—with a slider. These settings don't transfer to the iPod.

- **Sound Enhancer.** This feature is a kind of audio filter that can expand and brighten the sound coming from iTunes tracks. It's worth playing with to see whether its results please you. These settings don't transfer to the iPod either.

- **Sound Check.** In Chapter 2, I talk about the Sound Check feature on the iPod and how you have to enable it. This preference is where you do that. The feature's job is to try to make volumes across all the songs in your library similar.

Sharing

iTunes allows you to easily share your music library or just specific playlists in it with other copies of iTunes running on a local network (and allows those iTunes libraries to be shared with you). You can share your library by enabling the Share My Library on My Local Network option. To seek out other iTunes shared libraries, enable the Look for Shared Libraries option.

Store

As the name implies, this preference is where you tell iTunes how to interact with the iTunes Store. Options include Automatically Check for Available Downloads, Automatically Download Prepurchased Content, Automatically Download Missing Album Artwork, and Use Full Window for iTunes Store. All options but the last one are enabled by default.

Parental

Not all music and video is appropriate for all ages. Within the Parental preference, you can disable podcasts, radio, the iTunes Store (though optionally allow access to iTunes U), and shared libraries, as well as restrict content—certain movies, TV shows, and applications, and explicit material—from the iTunes Store.

Advanced

The Advanced preference is where you tell iTunes the location of your media files and how to organize them. In Chapter 8, I put this preference to good use in shifting an iTunes Library from a cramped startup drive to a more expansive external drive.

Working with the Info window

I talk about tagging a fair amount in this chapter. By *tagging,* I don't mean playing the kids' game, but practicing the subtle art of marking files with identifying bits of information (such as title, artist, album, and genre) so that you can locate and organize them more easily. You do all this in an item's Info window.

To produce an Info window, just select any hunk of media in your iTunes Library—such as a song, video, or podcast—and choose File > Get Info. The resulting window contains several tabs. For purposes of this chapter, the important ones include the following.

Tag, You're It

So how does iTunes know about tracks, artists, albums, and genres? Through something called *ID3 tags*. ID3 tags are just little bits of data included in a song file that tell programs like iTunes something about the file—not just the track's name and the album it came from, but also the composer, the album track number, the year it was recorded, and whether it's part of a compilation.

These ID3 tags are the key to creating great Smart Playlists. To view this information, select a track and choose File > Get Info. Click the Info tab in the resulting window, and you'll see fields for all kinds of things. You may find occasions when it's helpful to change the information in these fields. If you have two versions of the same song— perhaps one is a studio recording and another is a live recording—you could change the title of the latter to include *(Live)*.

A really useful field to edit is Comments. Here, you can enter anything you like and then use that entry to sort your music. If a particular track would be great to fall asleep to, for example, enter **sleepy** in the Comments field. Do likewise with similar tracks, and when you're ready to hit the hay, create a Smart Playlist that includes "Comment is sleepy." With this technique under your belt, you can create playlists that fit particular moods or situations, such as a playlist that gets you pumped up during a workout.

Summary

Should a stranger stop you in the street and demand the format, bit rate, location of a particular track in your iTunes Library, this tab is where you'd look. Additionally, you'll discover the track's name, artist, album, sample rate, modification date, play count, and last played date in the Summary tab.

Info

This tab is where all the tagging business takes place. Here, you find fields for such information as name, artist, album, composer, comments, year, and track number, as well as a Genre menu (**Figure 4.10**). iTunes is pretty good about filling in this information for you, but at times, you may need to tag your own music—when iTunes doesn't recognize a ripped CD, for example, or when you've ripped someone else's mix CD and iTunes can't identify its tracks.

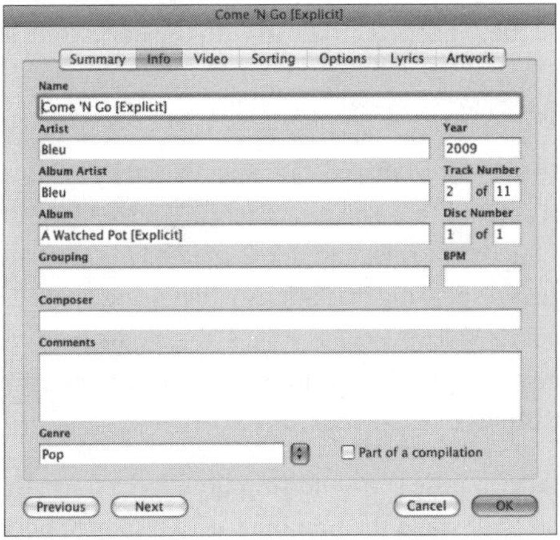

Figure 4.10

An Info window.

Video

When you import TV episodes from sources other than the iTunes Store, that video may lack the proper tags—show name, season, and episode number, for example. The Video tab contains fields for exactly that information.

Sorting

Tracks can be sorted by their real name, artist, album artist, album, composer, and show—or by their sort name, sort artist, sort album artist, sort album, sort composer, and sort show. Why? Suppose that you really like Willie Nelson. As you probably know, Willie has performed duets with every living artist born between 1925 and 1994—sometimes on his albums and sometimes on the duet partner's album. If you want to listen to all-Willie-all-the-time, you might track down all those duet tracks that aren't on Willie's own albums and assign *Willie Nelson* as the sort artist for those tracks. Do that, and when you sort tracks by artist or search for *Willie Nelson*, you'll find these tracks bunched in with the tracks from Willie's albums.

Options

Within the Options tab, you can adjust a track's volume so that it's louder or softer, choose an equalizer (EQ) preset (see the nearby sidebar "EQ and the iPod"), select an item's media type, and choose a VoiceOver language (for speaking track titles when using an iPod nano or shuffle that supports VoiceOver). For videos, the media type will be music video, movie, TV show, podcast, or iTunes U; for audio files, it will be music, podcast, iTunes U, audiobook, or voice memo.

You can also impose start and stop times on a track. This feature is useful when you can't stand the first minute of a song or podcast and want to skip that minute automatically whenever you play the track. To do that, enable the Start Time option and then enter **1:00** in the text box.

You'll also see the Remember Playback Position, Skip When Shuffling, and Part of a Gapless Album options. The first two options are particularly useful for audiobook chapters that you may have ripped. You want to be able to pick up listening where you left off in a 30-minute chapter, and you don't want your iPod randomly playing the third chapter of *Harry Potter and the Usurious Audiobook Purchase* when you're working out.

The last option, Part of a Gapless Album, overrides any crossfade setting that you've applied to a song, preventing songs that should naturally flow together (think *Dark Side of the Moon* or concert recordings) from being crossfaded.

Finally, cock a keen eye at the Rating field in the middle of the tab. Here, you can rate your tracks with one to five stars. (You can also rate tracks by clicking the Rating column next to a track's name, as well as by selecting a track and choosing a rating from the Rating submenu of the File menu.) Rating your media now is helpful for creating Smart Playlists later, basing those playlists on songs and videos you enjoy.

EQ and the iPod

Having EQ built into iTunes and the iPod is great, but the interaction between iTunes and the iPod in regard to EQ is a little confusing. Allow me to end that confusion.

In iTunes, you can assign an EQ setting to a song individually by clicking the song, pressing Command-I (Mac) or Ctrl+I (Windows), clicking the Options tab, and then choosing an EQ setting from the Equalizer Preset menu. When you move songs to your iPod, these EQ settings move right along with them, but you won't be able to use them unless you configure the iPod correctly.

(continued on next page)

EQ and the iPod (continued)

If, for example, you have EQ switched off on the iPod, songs that have assigned EQ presets won't play with those settings. Instead, your songs will play without the benefit of EQ. If you set the iPod's EQ to Flat, the EQ setting that you preset in iTunes will play on the iPod. If you select one of the other EQ settings on the iPod (Latin or Electronic, for example), songs without EQ presets assigned in iTunes will use the iPod EQ setting. Songs with EQ settings assigned in iTunes will use the iTunes setting.

If you'd like to hear how a particular song sounds on your iPod with a different EQ setting, start playing the song on the iPod, navigate to Settings > EQ, and then select one of the EQ settings. The song will immediately take on the EQ setting you've chosen, but this setting won't stick on subsequent playback. If you want to change the song's EQ more permanently, you must do so in iTunes.

Lyrics

You recall that your iPod can display lyrics, right? This tab is where you enter them. Regrettably, lyrics don't come with tracks that you purchase from the iTunes Store (no, not even with the premium-priced iTunes LPs that I discuss in Chapter 5). You're welcome to enter the lyrics by hand or search for them online. Music publishers have cracked down on Web sites that offer free lyrics, however, so these words are more difficult to find than they once were.

Artwork

iTunes is more than happy to seek out album artwork for you, but it locates artwork only for albums that are available from the iTunes Store. If you import an album that can't be had from the Store, a generic icon appears in Grid and Cover Flow views. You can add your own artwork simply by dragging a graphic file into the artwork field in the Artwork tab.

tip You can tag multiple files simply by selecting more than one file and choosing File > Get Info. A Multiple Item Information window appears, and you can add tags therein for such things as artist, album, composer, comments, genre, artwork, and rating. This feature is handy for adding one piece of album artwork to a group of tracks.

note The next few pages don't apply to the iPod shuffle, as its iTunes interface is significantly different from the one used for other iPod models. Because it *is* so different, I've chosen to devote the latter portion of this chapter to the shuffle.

Setting iPod Preferences

Now that your media is organized, it's time to put it on your 'pod. The conduit for moving music, podcasts, audiobooks, videos, and (for some models) applications and games to the iPod is iTunes—which, fortunately, can be fairly flexible in the way it goes about the process.

You have several ways to configure iTunes so that your iPod is updated when you want it to be. It's just as possible to configure iTunes so that only the music and videos you want are copied to your iPod. The key is the iPod Preferences window.

To start, plug your iPod into your computer, and launch iTunes. (By default, iTunes launches when you connect the iPod.) The iPod appears under the Devices heading in iTunes' Source list (**Figure 4.11** on the next page). To open the iPod Preferences window, select the iPod in the Source list.

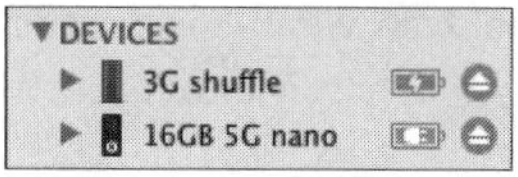

Figure 4.11

Two iPods in iTunes' Source list.

```
▼ DEVICES
  ▶ ▌  3G shuffle          🔋  ⏏
  ▶ ▌  16GB 5G nano        🔋  ⏏
```

Within the iPod Preferences window, you'll find nine tabs if you have a 5G iPod, 3G or 4G iPod nano, or any iPod classic: Summary, Music, Movies, TV Shows, Podcasts, iTunes U, Photos, Contacts, and Games. If you have a 5G iPod nano and have established a Nike+ account because of the pedometer, you'll see a tenth tab called Nike + iPod. If you have a color iPod that doesn't offer video (including 1G and 2G iPod nanos), the Movies, TV Shows, and Games tabs will be absent. For monochrome iPods, the Photos tab will also be missing.

At the bottom of the window, you'll see the Capacity bar (**Figure 4.12**), a thermometerlike display that details how much media is on your iPod. With any of today's display-bearing iPods plugged into your computer, you'll see entries for Audio, Video, Photos, Games, Other (data such as files you've copied to the iPod, notes, contacts, and calendars), and Free.

Figure 4.12

iTunes' Capacity bar.

| Capacity 14.98 GB | Audio 5.98 GB | Video 1.56 GB | Photos 758.3 MB | Games 69 MB | Other 524.3 MB | Free 6.12 GB |

Here's how the tabs shake out.

Summary

In iTunes 7 and later, the Summary tab (**Figure 4.13**) provides such details about your iPod as its name, capacity, software version number, serial number, and format (Macintosh or Windows). It also tells you the version of the iPod software it's running and offers you the option to update that software if newer software is available or to restore your iPod (essentially, erase its contents and give it a new operating system). I cover the ins and outs of restoring your iPod in Chapter 9.

Figure 4.13
The Summary tab.

Open iTunes When This iPod Is Attached

Most likely, you're going to want to sync or otherwise muck with your iPod when you plug it into your computer. This option saves you the trouble of launching iTunes manually.

Sync Only Checked Songs and Videos

This option gives you fine control of which files you sync to the iPod. Checking the box for this option lets you prevent files from loading onto the iPod by unchecking the small check boxes next to their names in playlists and library lists.

tip   Care to check or uncheck all the songs in a playlist at the same time? On the Mac, hold down the Command key and click any check box in the playlist. In Windows, hold down the Ctrl key and do the same thing. When you uncheck a box, all boxes will be unchecked; check a box, and all boxes will be checked.

Manually Manage Music and Videos

This small option offers a lot of power. To understand its usefulness, it's helpful to know that by default, when you sync iTunes and the iPod, iTunes moves only the files you ask it for onto the iPod and erases everything else from the device. This arrangement can be a real bother if you've moved your iPod from one computer to another and the contents of the second computer don't match those of the first.

Managing files manually allows you to add music (and videos, for compatible iPods) to your iPod without erasing any other media. When you select this option, all the playlists on your iPod appear below the iPod's icon in the iTunes Source list. (For the sake of simplicity, I'll say that the Music, Movies, TV Shows, Podcasts, and Audiobooks entries count as playlists.)

To add media files to the iPod manually, just select them in one of iTunes' playlists, and drag them to the iPod's icon in the Source list or to one of the iPod's standard (not Smart) playlists. You can also drag files from your computer's desktop directly to the iPod, which copies the media to the iPod but not to your iTunes Library.

Optionally, you can add songs by genre, artist, or album by using iTunes' browser. To do so, follow these steps:

1. In iTunes, choose View > Show Column Browser (Command-B in Mac OS X, Ctrl+B in Windows).

   An Artists pane appears between iTunes' Source list and the main window. By choosing View > Column Browser, you can choose to show (or hide, if they're shown) Genre and Albums columns as well.

2. Click an entry in one of the columns.

   If you want to copy all the Kate Bush songs in your iTunes Library to the iPod, for example, click Ms. Bush's name in the Artists column. To copy all the reggae tunes to the iPod, select Reggae in the Genres column.

3. Drag the selected item to the iPod's icon in the Source list or to a playlist you've created on the iPod.

To remove songs from the iPod, select the songs you want to remove
within the iPod entry in the Source list; then press your keyboard's Delete
key (or Control-click on the Mac or right-click for Windows, and choose
Clear from the contextual menu). Mac users can also drag the songs to
the Trash.

note   When you remove songs from your iPod, you don't remove them from
your computer. Unless you select a song in your iTunes Library and
delete it, the song is still on your hard drive.

You can even copy entire playlists to other playlists by dragging one playlist icon on top of another. This method works for both iTunes and iPod
playlists, though you can't drag a playlist on the iPod to an iTunes playlist
and expect the songs to copy over. Under most circumstances, tracks
on the iPod don't copy to your computer (unless you know the tricks
detailed in Chapter 8).

But wait—there's more. iTunes 9 lets you expose an Artwork column.
To reveal it, either click the small, right-pointing triangle that appears
just to the left of the Name column in List view or choose View > Show
Artwork Column. This column holds the leftmost position in iTunes' main
window and displays an album's artwork with the album's track names
in the next column to the right. This view is handy because you can click
the album artwork and drag it to the iPod, thus copying all the files on
the album to the device.

Want more? Okay, how about two additional views: Grid and Cover Flow?
Click the second button in the View palette at the top of the window to
see Grid view; Cover Flow view appears when you click the third button.
When you click the Grid button, you can view your music in Albums,

Artists, Genres, or Composers view. You choose these views by entering Grid view and then choosing Grid Views from the View menu.

tip There's another way to select these views. Choose View > Grid View, and select the Show Header command. When you choose Show Header, a bar appears above the covers that includes Albums, Artists, Genres, and Composers buttons, as well as a slider for increasing or decreasing the size of the artwork. If you tend to use Grid view and often want to switch views, using the Header buttons is mighty convenient.

These views work this way.

Albums. Each album cover in the selected entry (music or a playlist) is displayed (**Figure 4.14**). Mouse over the cover, and a Play Album entry appears. Click the Play symbol in this icon, and the album begins playing from the first track. Double-click an album cover, and a page opens that displays the album cover and the tracks on the album.

Figure 4.14
Albums displayed in Grid view.

tip   When you choose to view your music by album in Grid view, you have an additional sorting option. Choose View > Sort Album, and you'll find that you can sort albums by title, artist, genre, year, and rating. Then you can sort further by ascending or descending alphabetical order and, within each artist entry, by title, year, or rating. *Say what!?* Yes, it's confusing. Choose to sort by Artist, and you'll find all your David Bowie albums lined up sorted by the letter *D*, not *B*. (Like I said, it's confusing.)

note   If iTunes can't find the album artwork for a particular album, the cover shows a generic icon of two eighth notes.

Artists. When you select Artists, you'll still see album covers, but those covers will be grouped by artist. If you have tracks from more than one album by an artist, select an artist and roll your mouse horizontally over the cover; the album covers will change to reflect all the artist's album entries. A Play Artist entry also appears. Click the Play symbol in it, and iTunes begins playing the first track from the first album title, sorted alphabetically.

If you don't care for the idea of displaying all your Springsteen albums under a single icon and, instead, would like to see all the album covers separately but together, feel free to view by album and then use the sort-by-artist-within-albums tip I just offered.

Genres. Seeking a quick way to find all the World music in your iTunes Library? Select the Genres entry, and you'll see the selected playlist's music categorized by genre. (Those songs must have their Genre tag filled in to appear in this view, however. See the sidebar "Tag, You're It" earlier in this chapter for more information on tags.) For common genres, you'll see custom icons provided by Apple—Rock, Soundtrack, and World, for example. If tracks have a less-common genre type assigned to them— such as Ska, Metal, or Fusion—you'll see the album cover for a track tagged with that genre or with iTunes' generic eighth-notes icon.

As in Artists and Albums views, select an icon and move your mouse over it horizontally, and album covers appear. Click the Play symbol within the Play Genre entry that appears over selected icons to play all the music within that genre. Music is organized alphabetically by the artist's first name.

Composers. You know the drill by now. Tracks are organized by composers when those tracks contain a Composer tag. If not, you'll find the remaining tracks listed under Unknown Composer. Click the Play symbol in the Play Composer entry to play. Tracks are organized first by artist and then by album title. If you choose the leader of The Who, Pete Townshend, his solo albums come first in alphabetical order; then come The Who's albums in alphabetical order.

Cover Flow view is kind of a lazy-Susan affair that represents your library as a series of covers (**Figure 4.15**). You can move music from these views to your iPod simply by dragging the cover art from the view to the iPod's icon. The contents of that album, video, or podcast will be transferred to the iPod.

Figure 4.15
Cover Flow view.

Enable Disk Use

The iPod is, at heart, an elegant storage device that happens to play music (and in some cases, slideshows and videos too). You can mount all iPods (except the iPod touch) as a hard drive on your computer by enabling this option. When the iPod is mounted, you can use it just like a hard drive; copy files to it as you desire.

Voice Feedback (5G iPod nano and 3G iPod shuffle only)

The 5G iPod nano and 3G iPod shuffle have the ability to talk back to you. Specifically, they can recite the names of the devices' menus and commands (nano) as well as playlists, tracks, artists, and albums (both nano and shuffle). For that to happen, you must switch on the iPod's Voice Feedback feature.

The 5G iPod nano includes three options under the Voice Feedback heading:

- **Enable VoiceOver.** Enable this option, and you'll be prompted to download the VoiceOver Kit for the language your computer speaks (as determined by the language preferences set on your Mac or PC). Then sync your iPod. When you click the iPod's Center button while a track is playing, the music will fade a little, and a voice will announce the track's name and artist.

- **Enable Spoken Menus.** When Spoken Menus is enabled in iTunes and on your iPod, the name of every item the 5G iPod nano encounters will be spoken. This feature isn't for everyone, as it's somewhat intrusive, but if you're vision-impaired or blind, it's priceless.

  It's also worthwhile to switch on when you're driving with an iPod. Taking your eyes off the road to navigate an iPod's interface is a very bad idea, and now, thanks to Spoken Menus, you can navigate the device without looking at it.

> **tip**
>
> As I mention in Chapter 2, you can switch Spoken Menus off in the General screen, which is accessible from the nano's Setting screen.

■ **Use System Voice Instead of Built-In Voice.** If you don't care to use the voice that comes with the VoiceOver Kit that iTunes downloads, you can enable this option, and the iPod will speak using the voice currently set in your computer's speech preference. For the Mac, you'll find this setting by choosing System Preferences from the Apple menu or the Dock. On a Windows PC, look in Control Panels.

The Perfect Dismount

It's not a great idea to unplug a click-wheel iPod or iPod shuffle from your computer unceremoniously. For one thing, your computer's operating system will complain. Worse, your iPod may not have all the media you wanted it to have if it was busy doing something at the time.

To unmount your iPod properly, click the Eject icon next to the iPod's name in the Source list, or right-click (Control-click on the Mac) the iPod and choose Eject from the menu that appears. Alternatively, Mac users can switch to the Finder and drag the iPod to the Trash; when its icon disappears from the Desktop, you can unplug your iPod. Windows users can invoke the Safely Remove Hardware command from the notification area.

Music

The Music tab (**Figure 4.16**) contains options for syncing music and music videos to your iPod. With iTunes 9, Apple has completely redone the interface in this and other media windows, making it easier to get exactly the media you want onto your iPod.

Figure 4.16

The Music tab.

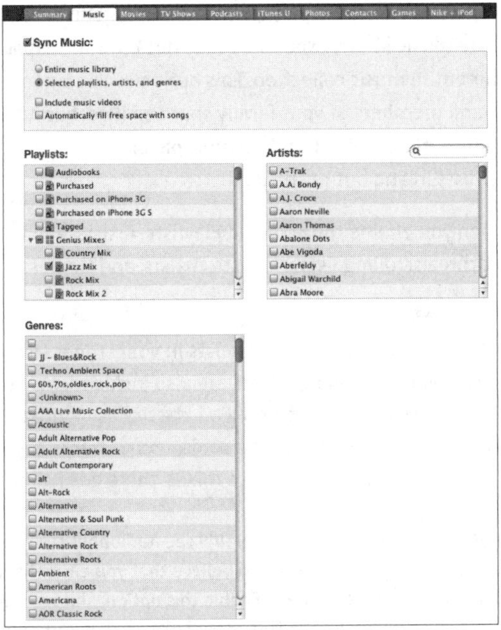

Enabling the Sync Music option tells iTunes that you'd like it to sync its music collection to the iPod automatically. If you've enabled the Manually Manage Music and Videos option in the Summary tab, enabling the Sync Music option overrides the Manual option (iTunes will ask you whether you're sure you want to do this). When you've chosen Sync Music, you then have the choice to sync your entire music library or just selected playlists, artists, and genres.

Any songs currently on the iPod that aren't in the iTunes Library or in the selected playlists are erased from the iPod.

Why choose selected playlists, artists, and genres rather than your entire music library? Your iPod may not have the capacity to hold your entire music collection. This option is also a good one to use when several members of your family share an iPod, because it allows you to chunk a music collection into multiple playlists and then rotate those playlists in and out of the iPod.

When you enable the Selected Playlists, Artists, and Genres option, you get three scrolling lists: Playlists, Artists, and Genres.

■ **Playlists**

This list includes all the playlists in your iTunes Library. If you have a 5G iPod nano, Genius Mixes are also included. (As I've told you, Genius Mixes aren't supported on iPod classics as I write this chapter.) Bear in mind that each Genius Mix contains 250 tracks. If you choose to sync more than a couple of these mixes, there goes all your iPod's storage.

tip At the top of this list, you'll see Audiobooks with no entries below it, which may lead you to believe that you either have to sync all of your audiobooks or none of them. Enable this option, and you will indeed sync every audiobook that appears in this special playlist. You can sync individual audiobooks, however, by placing them in a separate playlist and then syncing that playlist or by choosing an audiobook's author from the Artists list to the right of the Playlists list.

To sync playlists to your iPod, just enable them in this Playlists list. If you created a folder full of playlists by choosing File > New Playlist Folder and then enabled that folder, all the playlists within the folder will be synced to your iPod.

■ **Artists**

An improvement that came with iTunes 9 is the ability to sync individual artists' work to your iPod easily. You do this via the Artists list. Just enable the artists whose music you want to copy to your iPod, and so it shall be when you sync the iPod.

> **note** Notice the Search field above the Artists list. If you have a large iTunes Library, you'll find that this Search feature is a godsend.

■ **Genres**

Another hat-tip to iTunes 9 for the Genres list. If the holidays are beckoning, and you'd like to add a little musical cheer to the mix, enable the Holiday option in the Genres list, and your iPod will be as full of holiday music as it and your iTunes Library allow. Better yet, when the seemingly endless cheer ends, you can get that stuff off your iPod quickly by unchecking that genre and choosing a less festive one.

> **note** If you've removed songs from your iTunes Library and want them to remain on your iPod when you sync it, you'll want to avoid the Selected Playlists, Artists, and Genres option and manage your music manually.

You'll see two additional options in this tab: Include Music Videos and Automatically Fill Free Space with Songs. Enable the first option, and any music videos in selected playlists will also be synced to your iPod. Turn the option off, and music videos will steer clear, even if they're part of a playlist. As for the second option, if you haven't chosen enough music, videos, podcasts, photos, contacts, calendars, and games to fill your iPod, enabling this option instructs iTunes to top off your iPod with music of its choosing.

Movies

The Movies tab has been rejiggered in iTunes 9 as well. As with the Music tab, you can sync all your movies simply by checking the Sync Movies box and leaving the option below it set to automatically include all movies.

You can add a layer of choice by choosing one of the options from the Automatically Include pop-up menu. These options include syncing the 1, 3, 5, or 10 movies most recently added to iTunes; the 1, 3, 5, or 10 most recent unwatched movies (stuff that you haven't seen and added not all that long ago); or the 1, 3, 5, or 10 least recently unwatched movies (unwatched movies that are starting to gather dust in your iTunes Library).

When you choose one of these options, you're not committed to syncing only those movies. Below, you'll see all the movies in iTunes' Movies playlist with check boxes next to their titles. To sync any of these movies as well, just check their boxes (**Figure 4.17**).

Figure 4.17
The Movies tab.

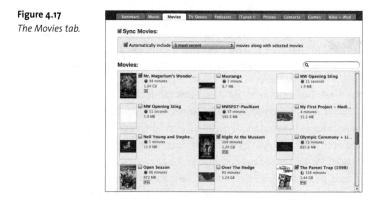

To be far more particular about the movies that are placed on your iPod, clear the Automatically Include check box. When you do, you see a list of all the movies in iTunes' Movies playlist, plus a list of all the playlists that include movies. Now you can pick just those movies you want, as well as pull movies from playlists you've created that may have a mix of movies and music (such as the Purchased playlist, which contains movies, TV shows, and music that you've bought from the iTunes Store).

Again, if you enable the Sync Movies option, you undo the Manually Manage Movies and Videos setting if you've switched it on.

Working with
Supported Video Formats

Regrettably, you can't take just any video you pull from the Web or rip from a DVD and plunk it on your iPod. Your iPod has standards that the video must meet before iTunes will allow it to touch the device.

Specifically, the videos must be in either MPEG-4 or H.264 format and must fit within these limits:

MPEG-4

Resolution: 640 by 480 pixels

Data rate: Up to 2.5 Mbps

Frame rate: 30 fps (frames per second)

Audio: Up to 48 kHz

H.264

Resolution: 640 by 480 pixels

Data rate: Up to 1.5 Mbps

Frame rate: 30 fps

Audio: Up to 48 kHz

What? If you have experience encoding video, these numbers will make sense to you; if they have you confused instead, don't fret. You needn't bone up on this technology, because iTunes provides a way to make your videos compatible with iPod classics and iPod nanos. Here's how: Drag an unprotected video (one that *isn't* a copy-protected TV show or video and that you *haven't* purchased from the iTunes Store) onto the Library entry in iTunes' Source list.

(continued on next page)

Working with
Supported Video Formats (continued)

If the video is compatible with iTunes, it will be added to the library; if not, the dragged icon will zip back to its original location. If the video isn't compatible, you can convert it with a utility such as Roxio Crunch, available for Windows and Macintosh for $40 (www.roxio.com), or the free, Intel-only Video Monkey (http://videomonkey.org).

Some videos that play in iTunes may be encoded at resolutions or data rates too high for the iPod to handle. Those files won't sync with your iPod, but you can make them compatible. To do that, select a video (listed in the Movies or TV Shows entry within iTunes' Source list), and choose Advanced > Create iPod or iPhone Version. This command creates an iPod- and iPhone-compatible version of the video, which you can sync to your iPod.

Note that converting a video for iPod compatibility doesn't replace the original, so it's not a bad idea to rename the converted version—*Casablanca (iPod),* for example—so that you can identify and sync the right one.

TV Shows

The TV Shows tab (**Figure 4.18**) works similarly to the Movies tab. When Sync TV Shows is enabled along with Automatically Include All Episodes of All Shows, all your TV shows will be copied to your iPod when you sync it. But here again, you have the option to sync the 1, 3, 5, or 10 most recent, most recent unwatched, and least recent unwatched episodes of all the shows in your iTunes Library or selected shows.

Figure 4.18
The TV Shows tab.

> **tip** What's with this "least recent unwatched episodes" stuff? If you've downloaded a season of a TV series, you'd choose this option so that the shows sync in order from the beginning of the season to the end. If, instead, you chose the most recent unwatched episodes, playback would start with the last show and then work its way backward. (If that wouldn't spoil the suspense, I don't know what would!)

As with the Movies tab, you can clear the Automatically Include check box, select individual shows and episodes within those shows, and sync just those shows and episodes to your iPod. Here, too, you'll find a list that lets you sync shows that are stored within specific playlists.

Podcasts

What puts the *pod* in *podcast* is the iPod. Because people tend to listen to lots of podcasts, some of which tend to be long (their files therefore taking up significant amounts of room), iTunes' Podcasts tab (**Figure 4.19** on the next page) lets you manage which ones are synced to your iPod.

Figure 4.19
The Podcasts tab.

As in each one of these tabs, you have the option to not sync this content, but if you choose to, you have plenty of options. To get it all, just enable Sync Podcasts, and the option below it, by default, reads Automatically Include All Episodes of All Podcasts. If you have a lot of podcast episodes—as many of us do—be choosy by choosing the proper options. Click the All pop-up menu, and you'll see familiar options—1, 3, 5, or 10 recent, most recent unplayed, and least recent unplayed. Additionally, you'll find options for playing all unplayed; all new; the 1, 3, 5, or 10 most recent new; and the 1, 3, 5, or 10 least recent new. You can do this for all podcasts or just selected podcasts.

Or—and I know you've heard this before—clear the Automatically Include check box, and choose the podcasts and episodes you want to sync. And yes, you can include episodes from podcasts contained within playlists.

Note that video as well as audio podcasts are included here. Because video can consume a lot of storage space, be careful how you choose your video podcasts.

iTunes U

Not terribly long ago, Apple introduced iTunes U, which provides audio and video content from such providers as universities, American Public Media, the Library of Congress, and The Metropolitan Museum of Art. And it's all *free!* Download some of this content, and you'll see that it can be synced very much like podcasts (**Figure 4.20**).

Figure 4.20
The iTunes U tab.

Photos (color iPods only)

The Mac and Windows versions of the Photos tab differ slightly. Like so.

Macintosh

If you use a Mac, an iPod with a color display can sync photos with Apple's iPhoto and Aperture, as well as with your Photos folder or a different folder of your choosing. On that Mac, you also have the option to sync all iPhoto albums, events, and faces. Or you can enable the Selected Albums, Events, and Faces, and Automatically Include option (**Figure 4.21** on the next page). Do this, and Albums, Events, and Faces lists appear. You can select specific items from these lists, such as all Faces photos that contain a picture of your boyfriend.

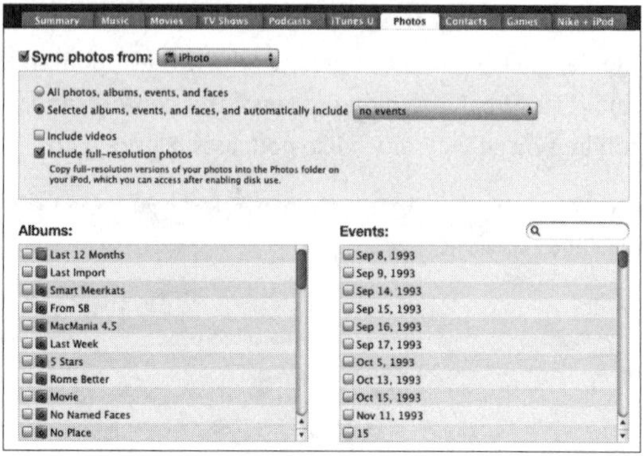

Figure 4.21
The Photos tab in the Mac version of iTunes.

With regard to events, iTunes offers the option to automatically include no events; all events; the most recent, 3, 5, 10, or 20 events; events from the past month; or events from the past 2, 3, 6, or 12 months. If you choose No Events, you can choose the specific events you want on your iPod from the Events list below. iTunes provides a Search field for making these events easier to find.

You also have the option to include videos that have been copied to your iPhoto library—videos you've shot with your 5G iPod nano, for example.

Aperture, a tool more often used by pros and advanced photo hobbyists, doesn't enjoy this level of support. Choose Aperture on a Mac version of iTunes, and you see but three options: All Photos and Albums, Selected Albums, and Include Full-Resolution Photos. Choose Selected Albums, and all your Aperture albums appear in a list below. As with iPhoto, you don't have the option to choose individual pictures from albums.

You can also select Choose Folder from the Sync Photos From pop-up menu. When you do, up pops a Change Photos Folder Location navigation window. Just traipse to the folder you want to pull pictures from, and click Open. When you do this, the folder you've chosen appears in the pop-up menu.

If you choose Pictures from this pop-up menu, the options below it change to All Photos and Albums and Selected Folders. The principles of iPhoto/Aperture import apply here as well. If you choose All Photos, iTunes rummages around in this folder and looks for compatible graphics files. If you choose Selected Folders, you can direct iTunes to look in only those folders that you select.

tip **This method is a good way to copy every picture from your hard drive to your iPod. As far as iTunes is concerned, your hard drive is just another folder. Select it as the source folder with the All Photos option selected, and iTunes grabs all the compatible graphics files it can find, converts them, and plunks them onto your iPod.**

This tab also include an Include Full-Resolution Photos option when you've plugged in any color iPod. It says what it means. When you enable it, iTunes creates a Photos folder at the root level of the iPod, and it hurls into that folder full-resolution versions of your photos rather than the slimmed-down photos that iPhoto displays. This option is primarily for transporting your photos; the iPod can't display them.

To access them, enable disk use on the iPod, locate the iPod on your Mac's Desktop, open the Photos folder, and then open the Full Resolution folder within. This folder is organized in a logical way. When you open the Full Resolution folder, you'll see a folder that bears the year the pictures were created. Within this folder are folders marked with the month of creation. Within one of these folders is a folder denoting the day of conception. So the folder hierarchy might look like this: Photos/Full Resolution/2009/10/28/*yourphotos*.

Windows

On a Windows PC, you can sync with your My Pictures folder, a different folder of your choosing, or photo albums created with Adobe Photoshop Elements 3 or later or Adobe Photoshop Album 2 or later. To do this, enable the Sync Photos From option, and from the pop-up menu that follows it, choose the source for your photos.

If you've installed Photoshop Elements (version 3 or later) or Photoshop Album on your PC, the Sync Photos From pop-up menu also contains entries for these programs, allowing you to import pictures from the albums that these programs create.

tip The tip I propose for copying all the pictures from your Mac to your iPod works in Windows as well. In this case, choose your C drive as the source. When you do, every compatible graphics file will be converted and copied.

The Windows version of iTunes also includes the option to include full-resolution versions of your photos.

Contacts

iTunes handles synchronization of contacts and calendars between your computer and iPod. The Contacts tab offers synchronization options for your computer's main contacts and calendars applications (**Figure 4.22**). From the Contacts tab on a Macintosh, you can choose to synchronize all your Apple Address Book contacts or just those contacts from selected groups. On a Windows PC, iTunes synchronizes Windows' Address Book (called Windows Contacts in Vista and Windows 7) or Microsoft Outlook

contacts in the same way—either all contacts or selected groups
of contacts. Each version of iTunes gives you the option to include
your contacts' photos.

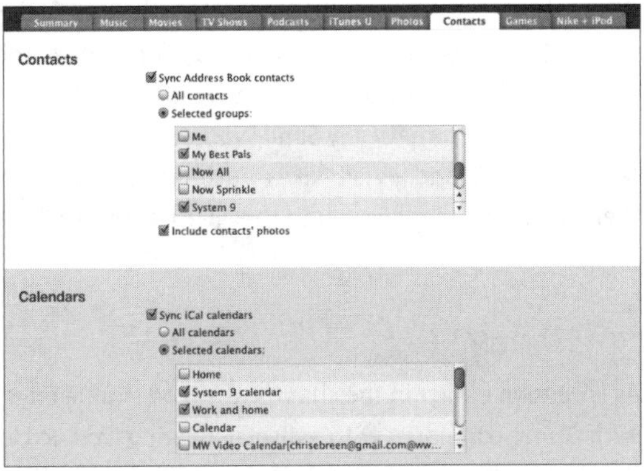

Figure 4.22
The Contacts tab.

Below the Contacts section of the tab, you'll spy the Calendars section,
which works similarly to Contacts. On a Mac, you can sync all your iCal
calendars or just selected calendars. On a Windows PC, you have these
same options for Microsoft Outlook calendars.

Games (5G iPod, 3G–5G iPod nanos, and iPod classics only)

The iTunes Store sells not only applications for the iPod touch and iPhone
through the App Store, but also games made specifically for click-wheel
iPods. Currently, the Store sells a small collection of games that are
compatible with the 3G–4G iPod nanos, iPod classics, and 5G iPod. Buy one
of these games, and you can play it on any (or all) of these iPod models.

The Games tab is where you choose which games to sync to your iPod.
Your choices are all games or selected games (from a list of purchased
games below).

Nike + iPod (5G iPod nano only)

If you've signed up for a Nike+ Active account and enabled the pedometer on your 5G iPod nano, when you attach your iPod, this tab appears. Within it, you see the number of workout history files waiting to be sent to Nike (if you haven't turned on the option to have the histories sent automatically). Below the Workout History area is the Nike+ area, which includes the Automatically Send Workout Data to Nike+ option; your Nike+ Login ID; and a Visit Nike+ button that, when clicked, launches your Web browser and takes you to the Nike+ Active Web site.

Configuring the 3G iPod shuffle

As I mention earlier in the chapter, the iPod shuffle interacts differently with iTunes compared with a display-bearing iPod. To begin with, because the shuffle lacks a screen, it doesn't need to offer options for synchronizing photos, videos, contacts, and calendars. The lack of a screen also means that navigating the device is more challenging than working your way through a display-bearing iPod. You are, in a very real sense, flying blind.

Also consider the shuffle's limited storage space. Because the 3G iPod shuffle hold just 2 GB or 4 GB, you don't have a lot of extra room for storing large music files. iTunes can be configured to keep such files from being placed on your music player automatically.

With these limitations in mind, take a look at just what iTunes offers for the shuffle owner.

When you attach an iPod shuffle to your Mac or PC, by default, iTunes launches. When it does, the shuffle appears in the iTunes Source list under the Devices heading, just like any other iPod (save for the fact that its icon looks like a shuffle rather than a full-size iPod). Select that shuffle, and iTunes' main window shows four tabs: Summary, Music, Podcasts, and iTunes U.

Summary

This tab looks similar to the Summary tab for other iPods (**Figure 4.23**). Because it does, and because it offers similar options, I won't dwell on those options.

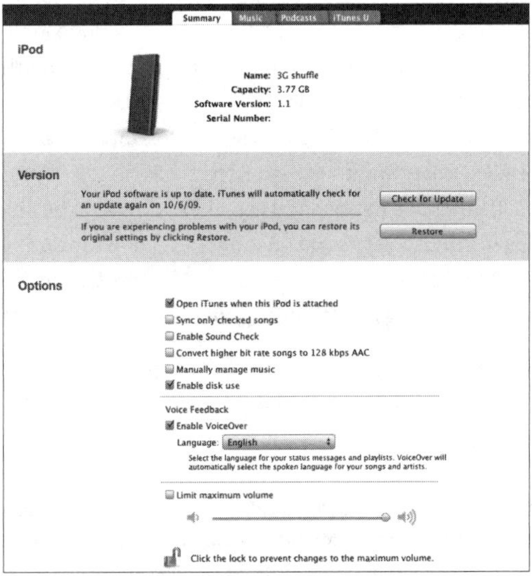

Figure 4.23

The Summary tab for a 3G iPod shuffle.

As do other Summary tabs, this one displays the name, capacity, software version, and serial number of the currently connected iPod shuffle. In the Version area below, you see the Check for Update and Restore buttons. As their names imply, the first, when clicked, checks for software updates for your iPod, and the second restores the iPod to its factory settings—meaning a brand-new copy of the latest software and all media wiped off the iPod.

In the Options area, you see several options that I've already discussed: Open iTunes When This iPod Is Attached, Sync Only Checked Songs, Enable Sound Check, Manually Manage Music, and Enable Disk Use.

There's also an option titled Convert Higher Bit Rate Songs to 128 Kbps AAC. As I've said, these iPods don't have a lot of storage capacity. If you want to get a lot of music on this iPod, it's a good idea to ensure that the files you load on it are on the slim side. Enabling this option will help because (as you recall from the "Import Business: File Formats and Bit Rates" sidebar earlier in this chapter) the lower the bit rate, the smaller the file. Converting those 256 Kbps tracks to 128 Kbps cuts their size in half. If you have particularly keen hearing, you'll be able to tell the difference if you use very good headphones (I don't include those included with the iPod among them). But quite honestly, most people—particularly those using Apple's headphones—can't tell the difference.

Below these options are the Voice Feedback option and the Enable VoiceOver check box, which work just the way they do with the 5G iPod nano.

note Disabling Enable VoiceOver doesn't mean that you're ridding the shuffle of Spoken Menus. Switch this option off, and the iPod will still announce the names of playlists when you click and hold the headset's Center button. What you lose is the iPod's ability to recite the names of songs and artists when you briefly click and hold the headset's Center button and skip back or forward.

At the bottom of this tab are the Limit Maximum Volume option and slider. On display-bearing iPods, you can limit the iPod's maximum volume directly on the iPod. Not so with the iPod shuffle. If you want to reduce its maximum volume (as you may want to do before handing the iPod over to a child who might be tempted to destroy his hearing), enable this option, and the volume indicator moves to the center of the slider.

Click the Lock icon at the bottom of the tab, and you'll be prompted for a password (and confirmation of that password). This option locks the iPod so that its volume can't be adjusted past this limit without the password.

Music

You've been here before. Enable the Sync Music option, and you're offered the choice to sync your entire music library or selected playlists, artists, and genres (with lists of those playlists, artists, and genres appearing below). The Automatically Fill Free Space with Songs option lives here too.

The Hidden Autofill Feature

If you owned an iPod shuffle before the current 3G iPod shuffle, you're likely wondering where the Autofill feature went. With this feature, you selected a playlist, and iTunes filled your iPod shuffle from the contents of that playlist. This feature appears to have disappeared from the 3G shuffle.

Ah, but appearances can be deceiving. Autofill still exists—and better yet, it can be used with other iPod models. To make it appear, do this:

1. In the Summary tab, enable the Manually Manage Music option.

2. Click the triangle next to the icon of your iPod in iTunes' Source list to expose the playlists (Music, Podcasts, Audiobooks, and so on).

3. Select the iPod's Music entry (the one that appears just below its name in iTunes' Source list).

4. Whoop for joy when you see three new items at the bottom of the iTunes window: the Autofill From pop-up menu, the Settings button, and the Autofill button.

(continued on next page)

The Hidden Autofill Feature (continued)

This is what they do:

Autofill From pop-up menu

As I've already mentioned, you can autofill an iPod from any play-list in iTunes. This pop-up menu is where you choose that playlist (**Figure 4.24**). If you want your iPod to be filled from every bit of your music library, just accept the default setting, Music.

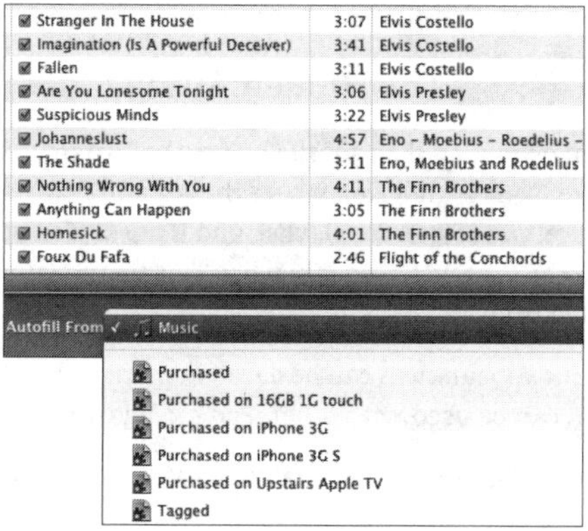

Figure 4.24
Choosing a playlist to autofill from.

☑ Stranger In The House	3:07	Elvis Costello
☑ Imagination (Is A Powerful Deceiver)	3:41	Elvis Costello
☑ Fallen	3:11	Elvis Costello
☑ Are You Lonesome Tonight	3:06	Elvis Presley
☑ Suspicious Minds	3:22	Elvis Presley
☑ Johanneslust	4:57	Eno – Moebius – Roedelius –
☑ The Shade	3:11	Eno, Moebius and Roedelius
☑ Nothing Wrong With You	4:11	The Finn Brothers
☑ Anything Can Happen	3:05	The Finn Brothers
☑ Homesick	4:01	The Finn Brothers
☑ Foux Du Fafa	2:46	Flight of the Conchords

Autofill From ✓ 🎵 Music

🎵 Purchased
🎵 Purchased on 16GB 1G touch
🎵 Purchased on iPhone 3G
🎵 Purchased on iPhone 3G S
🎵 Purchased on Upstairs Apple TV
🎵 Tagged

Settings button

Click this button, and you discover a few options (**Figure 4.25**). The first, Replace All Items When Autofilling, does what it suggests; any music on the iPod is removed and replaced with autofilled music. Leaving this box checked is a good way to help ensure that you get a fresh crop of music next time you listen to your shuffle. It's not such a good choice, however, if you want to keep some selections on the shuffle (podcasts, for example) and remove others.

The Hidden Autofill Feature (continued)

Figure 4.25
Autofill Settings window.

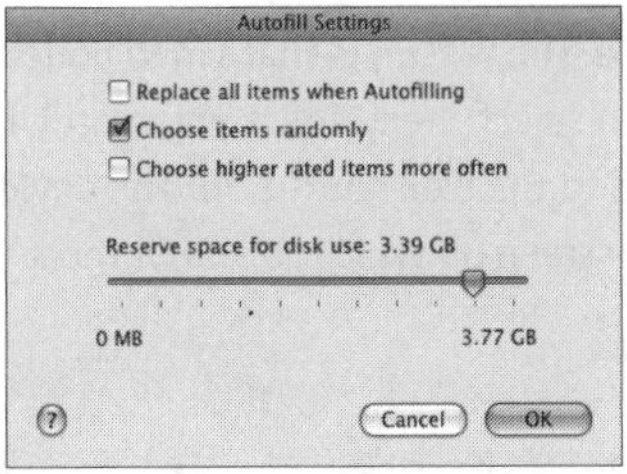

The second option, Choose Items Randomly, grabs any old tracks in the selected playlist and biffs them onto your iPod. Leave this option off, and the iPod will be filled with as much of the playlist as will fit, starting with the first track and syncing in order.

The third option, Choose Higher Rated Items More Often, is iTunes' way of giving your iPod more of the music you like. I mean, honestly, what's the use of putting music that you loathe on your iPod? If you haven't thought of a good reason for rating your audio files, now you have one. Assign a rating of four or five stars to your favorite tracks, and those tracks are more likely to be moved to your shuffle when this option is enabled.

Finally, at the bottom of this window, you see a slider that reads Reserve Space for Disk Use. The slider below runs from 0 MB to the capacity of your iPod—111.61 GB for a 120 GB iPod classic, for example. With this slider, you designate how much space you're willing to hand over for music storage when autofilling.

Autofill button

This is the "Go ahead and do it" button. Click it, and iTunes will begin autofilling your music using the playlist and settings you've chosen.

Podcasts

This tab is exactly the same as the Podcasts tab that appears when any other iPod is jacked into your computer—which can be a little deceiving with the iPod shuffle. The reason is that video podcasts also appear in this tab, and you can select them. Try as you might, however, you can't sync these podcasts to the iPod shuffle, for the obvious reason that the shuffle provides no screen on which to watch those podcasts.

iTunes U

This option also looks exactly the same as the iTunes U tab that appears for other iPods, and the same caveat applies: Any iTunes U video content that you have can't be synced to an iPod shuffle.

5

The iTunes Store

Chapter 4 shows you how to put the music and video you own on your iPod. Now it's time to look at a cool way to obtain new media. And by *cool*, I can mean nothing other than Apple's online digital media emporium: the iTunes Store.

Apple eschewed the typical Internet-commerce model of creating a Web site that users access through a Web browser. Although this model works reasonably well for countless merchants, it invariably requires customers to slog through Web page after Web page to find and pay for the items they desire. Apple wanted a service as immediate as the experience of going to a media megastore, gathering the music and movies you want, and taking them to the counter.

To replicate this experience, Apple placed The Store inside an application that was already built for music browsing (and, later, video browsing) and that many of its customers were likely to be familiar with: iTunes.

In the following pages, I take you on a tour of The Store and show you the best ways to discover and purchase new media.

Prepare to Shop

Ready to shop? Great. First, make sure that you have the tools you need to get started. After you have those tools, I'll get you signed up with an account and then take you on an extensive tour of The Store.

What you need

Naturally, you need a Mac or a Windows PC and a copy of iTunes. It's not necessary to have an iPod to take advantage of The Store. Media purchased at The Store can be played on your computer; music can be burned to CD; and because Apple now sells music free of copy protection, the music you purchase there can be played on any device that supports the AAC format (discussed in Chapter 4).

Also, although you can access The Store via any Internet connection, you'll find it far more fun to shop with a reasonably speedy broadband connection. A 4-minute song weighs in at around 8 MB. Such a download takes next to no time over a DSL, cable, or fiber-optic connection but can be terribly slow over a poky Wi-Fi connection or—heaven forbid!—a slothlike dial-up modem. Even with a moderately fast broadband connection, you could wait up to an hour to download a full-length movie from The Store.

As these pages go to print, The Store is available in 77 countries. Which store you're allowed to purchase media from depends on the issuing country of your credit card. If you have a credit card issued in Germany, for example, you can purchase media only from the German iTunes Store (though you don't physically have to be in Germany to do this; again, the credit card determines where you can shop).

Sign on

You're welcome to browse The Store the first time you fire up iTunes, but to purchase media, you must establish an account and sign in. Fortunately, Apple makes the process pretty easy.

With your computer connected to the Internet, launch iTunes, and click the iTunes Store entry in iTunes' Source list; then click the Sign In button in the top-right corner of the iTunes window. If you have either an Apple ID and password or an AOL screen name and password, enter them and click the Sign In button; otherwise, click the Create New Account button.

When creating an account, you'll be required to agree to the iTunes Store's terms-of-service agreement, enter a valid email address, and create a password. Along the way, you'll enter some personal information so that Apple can identify you if need be.

Finally, you'll be asked for a credit-card number and your name, address, and phone number. Click Done and . . . you're done. You're now a member in good standing.

Navigate The Store's Floors: Main Page

As I tap out these words, The Store carries more than 10 million songs, a million podcasts, 3,000 TV shows, 2,500 films, 40,000 music videos, 75,000 iPod touch/iPhone applications, 20,000 audiobooks, and a trickle of iPod games. You needn't trudge through an alphabetical list of all these items. Instead, Apple offers you multiple ways to browse its catalog of goodies. In this section, I show you the floor plan of The Store's main page and the best ways to navigate it.

Main-page layout

The Store's main page is all about featured content and helping you find your way around (**Figure 5.1**). Accordingly, you'll see lots of images, large and small, that lead you to new and interesting music, movies, TV shows, audiobooks, and iPod touch/iPhone applications. Additionally, the page houses navigation controls and links for exploring various areas of The Store.

Figure 5.1
The Store's main page.

Quick Links and Top Charts

Along the right edge of the main page are a Quick Links area (which I talk about in greater depth later in the chapter) and a Top Charts area where you see links to the top 10 songs, music videos, albums, movies (for sale and for rent), and TV episodes and seasons.

Top promo banner

Across the top of the main page, you'll see a banner that changes from time to time, promoting hot new singles or albums, exclusive tracks, music videos, TV shows, applications, and movies.

New Releases

Below this banner is the New Releases section, which consists of side-scrolling panes. The topmost pane displays new albums and singles; you toggle between items by clicking the appropriate button. At the bottom of this pane is a scroll bar that you can click and drag to see more contents of the pane.

Next to the Albums and Singles buttons is a See All link that, when clicked, takes you to a page that lists all of the week's notable new albums or singles (depending on whether you clicked the Albums or Singles button before clicking Show All). Within this page, you can sort by Name, Release Date, or Featured by making a choice from the Sort By pop-up menu in the top-right corner.

More promos

Below New Releases is an area that promotes recent or upcoming releases—the single of the week, a movie you can preorder, and a pitch for new HD TV episodes, for example.

Genius Recommendations

Travel farther down to see the Genius Recommendations section, which offers recommendations based on the contents of your iTunes Library (if you've chosen to share that information with Apple, as I outline in Chapter 4). You can elect to see Music, Movies, or TV Shows recommendations by choosing one of these entries from a View pop-up menu on the right side of the Genius Recommendations area. When Music is selected, you'll see Album recommendations in a horizontal scrolling area to the left and a list of ten singles you might like on the right side of the page. You can preview these singles by hovering your cursor over a track until it adopts a gray hue and a blue Preview button appears to the left of the track's name. You can also click the Price/Buy button ($0.99, for example) to purchase the track.

note If you haven't purchased a particular kind of media from the iTunes Store—no movies, for example—you won't see recommendations for that media type, because Genius has nothing to base recommendations on.

This pane also features a See All link. Click it, and off you go to a pane that displays more recommendations. The interesting thing to note here is that The Store tells you *why* it's recommending something. Apparently because I like The Finn Brothers, for example, I will also enjoy Sister Hazel's *Absolutely*.

tip The Store welcomes your reactions to its recommendations. Below each recommendation are Thumbs Up and Thumbs Down icons. If you approve of The Store's suggestion that your love for Green Day earns a Weezer recommendation, by all means, click Thumbs Up. If, on the other hand, you can't believe that any entity—human or otherwise—would equate *Dexter* with Season 1 of *30 Rock*, click the Thumbs Down icon.

New movies and TV shows

Skip down another section, and you find recent additions to The Store's movie catalog. Again, this section is a side-scrolling pane with a See All link. Down one more section is a TV section that operates exactly the same way.

Previewing Media

Before I get too far into this chapter, I'd like to point out in this very obvious way that when you purchase media from The Store, you have a good idea of what you're getting. That method involves the Preview buttons scattered about the place.

Suppose that your favorite artist has just emerged from a very messy (and very public) divorce. You're in the mood for something upbeat, and you fear that with an album title along the lines of *That Dirty No-Good Cheatin' Skunk Is Dead to Me,* you, as listener, may be in for a rough ride. Fortunately, you needn't spend a nickel to discover exactly how low that artist will go.

Just hover your cursor over a track until its title turns bold black, the background adopts a blue/gray hue, and a blue Preview button appears next to the track's name. Click this Preview button, and you hear the first 30 seconds of a very angry song. Select another track, click its Preview button, and—oh, my heavens—now she's not only angry, but homicidal as well. You might want to give this one a pass and spend your hard-earned money on some perky Bananarama.

You can preview not only songs, but movies, TV shows, and audiobooks too. All movies offer a View Trailer button at the top of the window, which, when clicked, lets you watch the original theatrical trailer. TV episodes offer the same sort of Preview button that you find for music tracks. Click it, and a video window appears in which the preview plays. And an audiobook's page features a large gray Preview button. Audiobook previews last 90 seconds. Podcasts and iTunes U content comes without previews because, after all, it's free to begin with.

Featured media

After another row of featured items is an area that highlights a particular collection of media. As I write this chapter, for example, The Store is showcasing $7.99 reggae albums.

Free On iTunes

Finally, way down near the bottom of the page, is one of my favorite sections: Free On iTunes. As the name implies, every bit of media here is free. You'll find TV-show pilots, short films, featurettes (read: long movie previews), audiobook excerpts, and free singles.

Navigation links

At the very, very bottom of the main page is a collection of links to important areas of The Store. These links are divided into four categories: Explore, Features, Help, and Manage.

Explore

Below this heading is a list of The Store's main media sections: Music, Movies, TV Shows, App Store, Podcasts, Audiobooks, and iTunes U. Clicking one of these links takes you to the main page for that media type. (These links serve the same purpose as the headings in the navigation bar at the top of the page, which I discuss in short order.)

Features

Here, you find links to The Store's browser, celebrity playlists, HD movies, iTunes Essentials (collections of music that Apple believes goes well together), and a place to preorder upcoming movies.

Help

Look under this heading for iTunes support, iTunes tutorial videos, contact links, the App Store FAQ, help with movie rentals (where you'll go if a rental didn't reach you as it should have), and iTunes Pass (a feature for prepurchasing a band's upcoming content).

Manage

Manage provides links to your iTunes account information; the Redeem area, where you can redeem iTunes gift cards; My Wish List, where you can store links to items you're thinking about buying; and Change Country, where you can choose to shop at a different iTunes Store (but you'll need a credit card issued in that store's country to purchase anything).

What's the Cost?

At one time, you knew exactly what you'd pay when you visited the iTunes Store: 99 cents for a single music track and $9.99 for an album. With all the media now available in The Store and Apple's adoption of variable pricing for much of it, that situation has changed. Here's the rundown:

■ **Music.** Singles are priced at 69 cents, 99 cents, or $1.29. The most popular current tracks are $1.29. Albums cost $9.99 on average, but you can find bargains in the $7 and $8 range, as well as albums that cost $2 and $3 more. iTunes LPs (albums that contain enhanced material) are usually priced a few dollars more than the unenhanced versions. Albums that ship on two or more physical CDs cost quite a bit more, naturally.

■ **Music Videos.** Each video costs $1.99.

(continued on next page)

What's the Cost? (continued)

- **TV Shows.** In most cases, standard-definition TV episodes are $1.99 each. (Such HBO shows as *The Sopranos* and *Rome* cost $2.99 per standard-definition episode.) High-definition TV episodes cost $2.99.

  TV seasons are priced according to the number of episodes they contain and the format they're in: HD or standard definition. You sometimes get a break for buying a season, but more often than not, you pay the aggregate price of all the episodes.

- **Purchased movies.** Apple characterizes movies as being library (meaning *older*) or new. Standard-definition library titles are $9.99; new standard-definition titles are $14.99. As I write this chapter, all HD titles are $20. Similar to iTunes LPs, iTunes Extras movies contain bonus material. These movies cost $15.

- **Rental movies.** Standard-definition library titles are $2.99, and new library titles in standard definition are $3.99. Library HD rentals are $3.99, and new HD rentals are $4.99. After you download a rental movie, you have 30 days to watch it. After you start watching it, you have 24 hours to finish it; the movie is automatically removed from the iPod after that period. During those 24 hours, you can watch the movie as many times as you like.

- **Audiobooks.** The pricing of audiobooks is all over the map. You can find some for just over $10, whereas others can cost up to $50 (because, apparently, the real magic of the Harry Potter novels is that they can command these kinds of prices).

- **Podcasts and iTunes U.** Free.

Cruise the Navigation Bar

Apple doesn't expect you to shop only for items listed on the main page. You need a way to move easily to areas of The Store that interest you. That's the purpose of the navigation bar, which is always in view regardless of where you are (**Figure 5.2**). I discuss its many elements in the following sections, discussing in left-to-right order.

Figure 5.2 *The Store's navigation bar.*

Back and Forward buttons

These buttons serve a function similar to those of the same-named buttons in your Web browser. As you traipse through The Store, you can backtrack along your path by clicking the Back button. If you've gone back and would like to move forward along ground you previously trod, use the Forward button.

Home

As far as The Store is concerned, Home is the main page. Clicking this button takes you there.

Music

Hover your cursor over the Music entry, and you see a small down-pointing triangle, which indicates that a menu is eager to pop down and provide you options. Click that triangle, and sure enough, a menu appears. That menu includes Music Videos, iTunes Essentials, and Pre-Orders options, as well as a list of genres. Select Music Videos, and you're taken to an area of The Store that sells them. To find iTunes Essentials—The Store's greatest-hits packages—choose this item. Choosing Pre-Orders takes you to a collection of upcoming albums by popular artists.

Choose a genre entry—Classical, Rock, Reggae, or World, for example—and you're transported to a page that features music of that genre. These pages are arranged very much like The Store's main page but present music in different ways. Each genre page offers a New and Noteworthy area, but beyond that, you could see collections of live recordings, What's Hot, "What We're Listening To" recommendations, and classic recordings. Some pages also include music videos related to the genre. On the right side of each page are a Top Charts heading and, below it, the genre's top ten songs and albums.

If you simply click Music, you're taken to the main Music page, which includes a mix of music along with Genius Recommendations. The right side of this page has its own links.

Speaking of those links, longtime iTunes Store customers may fear that some of their favorite features—such as iMix, iTunes Essentials, and Celebrity Playlists—have disappeared simply because they've vanished from The Store's main page. Fear not. The music-centric items have been moved to the main Music page and now reside below the More in Music heading on the right side of the page (scroll down to see it).

For those who are unfamiliar with these music features, here's how the most significant ones shake out.

iTunes LP

These items, introduced with iTunes 9, are albums enhanced with bonus material such as photos, videos, liner notes, and lyrics (**Figure 5.3**). (Regrettably, the lyrics from these albums aren't transferred to your iPod.) This enhanced content is playable on your Mac or Windows PC, and the albums are generally priced a few dollars more than the unenhanced versions.

Figure 5.3
A collection of iTunes LPs.

iTunes Essentials

It makes sense that Apple would offer compilations of songs organized by artist or by some catchy sort of theme (Women in Bluegrass, Animation Classics, or Old Friends with New Albums, for example). Apple calls these compilations *iTunes Essentials*.

Yes, these collections are essentially Apple's own iMixes (which I cover shortly)—groups of songs that the folks who work at The Store think you'll like (**Figure 5.4** on the next page). Unlike most of The Store's other albums, these compilations don't give you a discount. If an iTunes Essential contains 25 songs priced at 99 cents each, you pay $24.75.

iTunes Essentials are offered in four configurations: The Basics, Next Steps, Deep Cuts, and Complete Set. As their names indicate, The Basics includes the most obvious songs that fit a particular theme; Next Steps offers slightly more obscure tracks; Deep Cuts hits the fringes; and Complete Set offers all songs in the previous three categories.

Figure 5.4
An iTunes Essentials collection.

iMix

iMix is your chance to inflict your musical values on the rest of the world by publishing a playlist of your favorite (or, heck, your least-favorite) songs. When you click the iMix link, you're taken to a page that contains three columns marked Top Rated, Most Recent, and Featured, all listing iMix playlists posted by fellow music lovers. Type a genre, artist name, or keyword (such as *summer* or *drive*) in the Search For field to narrow your choices, or just click an "album cover" to view the songs in an iMix (and buy them, if you like).

As enjoyable as it may be to view others' iMixes, creating your own is more fun. You can do so by following these steps:

1. Create a new playlist in iTunes, and give it a really cool name.

   The cooler the name, the more likely other people are to view your iMix.

2. Cruise through your iTunes Library, and drag into it songs you'd like to publish in an iMix.

note Your iMix can contain only songs available for purchase from The Store. If the iMix contains songs that aren't available at The Store, those songs won't appear in the published playlist.

3. Round out your list with songs at The Store that you don't own.

   An iMix doesn't require that you actually own the music you're recommending; you can drag previews of any song or audiobook from The Store into a playlist in iTunes' Source list. Feel free to add these previews to your iMix playlist.

4. Click the arrow to the right of your playlist's name.

   When you click this arrow, a dialog box asks whether you'd like to give the playlist as a gift or publish it as an iMix.

5. Click Create iMix.

   You'll be asked to sign in with your Apple ID. Then you'll be taken to The Store, and iTunes' main window will show you a picture of your iMix's album cover (a collage of album covers for the songs you've included).

6. Edit the title and description to suit your iMix (**Figure 5.5**).

Figure 5.5
Naming an iMix.

7. Click Publish and then click Done.

   Your iMix will be published to The Store, where it will remain for 1 year. You'll receive an email confirmation of the iMix's publication and a link to it. Click the link, and iTunes takes you to your iMix's page. Here, you have the option to advertise your iMix by clicking the Tell a Friend link.

Celebrity Playlists

If you'd like to know what rocks the world of a celebrity such as Robin Williams, Elizabeth Moss, Los Tigres del Norte, or Larry the Cable Guy (and yes, you'd be correct if you suggested "redneck rock" for Larry), click his or her link. The resulting page offers a list of tunes that the artist thinks worthy. You can preview and purchase songs—either individually or the entire list—directly from this page.

Just Added

To see lists of music added in the past 4 weeks, arranged by artist name, click this link.

Starbucks Entertainment

Apple has entered into partnership with Starbucks to sell music from Starbucks' music label. This section of The Store is reserved for this music and for music that goes well with a double wet nonfat soy cappuccino.

Nike Sport Mix

As I've hinted elsewhere in this book, Nike and Apple have teamed to pair music and athletic shoes. This section of The Store features mixes designed for the perfect workout. Each mix includes an opening narration that describes the kind of workout the mix is for, followed by the songs.

Live from Las Vegas at The Palms and Live From SoHo

These sections feature live recordings of concerts performed at the Palms Resort in Las Vegas and at Apple's New York SoHo store. Some concerts are audio only; others are videos.

Movies

The Movies entry also sports a menu. This one includes iTunes Extras, HD Movies, and New to Own, as well as its own list of genres, such as Action & Adventure, Comedy, Romance, and Western.

iTunes Extras

iTunes Extras are movies that contain not just the movie, but also the kind of extra content you find on DVDs—cast interviews, deleted scenes, documentaries, commentary tracks, and photo galleries, for example (**Figure 5.6**). As I write this chapter, just a few of these movies are available, but because they cost more than the other movies that The Store sells (meaning more profit for Apple and the movie companies), more are sure to come soon.

Figure 5.6
A collection of iTunes Extras movies.

HD Movies

This link takes you to high-definition (720p) movies for sale or rent from The Store.

note No, you can't play HD movies on your iPod; it supports standard definition movies only. When you purchase an HD movie, however, you also receive a version compatible with an iPod or iPhone. This bonus applies to purchases only; HD movie rentals don't include the standard-definition version.

New to Own

The New to Own section features recently released movies that you can purchase. Some are also available to rent.

Genre list

Select a genre in this list, and you'll be taken to a page that features movies within that genre. Elements include a New and Noteworthy section and a couple of collections of movies organized by theme— Screwball Comedies or Song and Dance, for example. The genre's top ten movie sales and movie rentals are listed along the right side of the pane.

Click the navigation bar's Movies button without invoking its menu, and off you go to The Store's main Movies page. Here are new movies for sale or rent, Genius Recommendations, movies collected by theme, and special offers. On the right side of the pane are the expected top-ten lists, as well as a More in Movies area with links to 99-cent movies of the week, movies under $5 and $6, highlighted collections (Disney, *Star Trek,* and James Bond, for example), and movies organized by rating. You'll also find a link to theatrical trailers here. Click that link, and you could easily spend the next couple of days watching the many movie previews offered by The Store.

TV Shows

The TV Shows menu resembles the Movies menu. Click the triangle, and you're presented with three options plus genre listings. In this case, those three options are HD TV, Shows Just Added, and Network & Studios. You undoubtedly have the idea about how these options work.

Worth mentioning is the fact that you can purchase individual episodes as well as full seasons from The Store. You can also purchase season passes for shows, which means that you pay now to preorder every episode that will come along during the season. When an episode becomes available, iTunes downloads it automatically. You'll find Buy Season Pass buttons on many currently running shows' pages.

Click the TV Shows button, and you're presented with the TV Shows main page, which is similar to the Music and Movies main pages (**Figure 5.7**).

Figure 5.7
The TV Shows main page.

note As with HD movies, when you purchase an HD TV episode, you also receive a standard-definition version that you can play on your iPod and/or iPhone.

App Store

You can't run iPod touch/iPhone applications on your click-wheel iPod or iPod shuffle, so I'll save this topic for my iPod touch and iPhone books.

Podcasts

Indeed, the three-plus-genres theme is alive and well in this menu, too. The first three entries this time are Audio Podcasts, Video Podcasts, and New Releases. The list of genres includes such entries as Arts, Health, Kids & Family, News & Politics, and—one of my favorites—Technology.

When you select a podcast (video or audio), you'll be taken to a page devoted to it. From this page, you can download single episodes (by clicking the Get Episode button that appears to the right of the podcast) or subscribe to the podcast (by clicking the Subscribe button).

When you click Get Episode, iTunes begins downloading the podcast, as evidenced by the spinning download icon next to the Downloads entry in iTunes' Source list. When the episode has downloaded, click the Podcasts entry in iTunes' Source list, and you'll see the name of the show below the Podcast heading. Click the triangle icon next to the show name, and you'll see the episode you downloaded below.

Next to a show's subject heading, you'll spy a Subscribe button (**Figure 5.8**). When you click this button or the Subscribe button in one of The Store's podcast pages, some previous episodes of the now-subscribed show will appear in the Podcasts pane, accompanied by a Get button next to each episode that, when clicked, allows you to retrieve the episode. If you want all the episodes offered, just click the Get All button next to the show's title. When new episodes become available, iTunes will download them automatically.

Figure 5.8

A podcast within iTunes' Podcasts area.

If you tire of receiving a particular show, just select its subject heading and then click the Unsubscribe button at the bottom of the iTunes window.

Audiobooks

Another menu, another three entries plus genres. The top three slots of this menu are Audiobook of the Month, New in Fiction, and New in Nonfiction. Click the Audiobooks entry itself, and you're whisked to the Audiobooks main page, complete with New & Noteworthy, top-ten lists, other entries promoting a particular genre of book—Sci-Fi & Fantasy, for example—and Staff Favorites. Along the right side of the page, you'll also find links to popular authors.

iTunes U

Surprise! The iTunes U menu, although indeed a menu, doesn't have three special entries at the top. Instead, it simply lists categories: Business, Engineering, Fine Arts, Health & Medicine, History, Humanities, Language, Literature, Mathematics, Science, Social Science, Society, and Teaching & Education. You can obtain this free content by individual episode (lecture? unit? thingie?); by entire course; or, in some cases, by subscribing to an ongoing series. When you download this material, it appears within the iTunes U category in iTunes' Source list.

Account

If you've signed into The Store, the last entry in the navigation bar will be Account, as denoted by your Apple ID (such as *jdoe@example.com*). This display is more than just a reminder of your ID. Mouse over it, and you see that darned triangle again. Click the triangle, and a menu appears that includes Account, Redeem, Wish List, and Sign Out. I discuss these options later in the chapter.

Click the Quick Links

Because The Store is an electronic emporium, you have the power to do things you couldn't dream of doing at a bricks-and-mortar store. The Quick Links area, in the top-right corner of each of The Store's pages, provides access to much of that power (**Figure 5.9**).

Figure 5.9

iTunes' Quick Links.

Quick Links

Redeem
Buy iTunes Gifts
Power Search
Browse
Account
Support

Genius Recommendations
My Wish List ①
My Alerts
Complete My Album
iTunes Plus 25+

Each section of The Store has its customized collection of Quick Links. For purposes of this section, you're interested only in those that appear when you're looking at the home page. There, you'll spy Redeem, Buy iTunes Gifts, Power Search, Browse, Account, Support, Genius Recommendations, My Wish List, My Alerts, Complete My Album, and iTunes Plus. They work this way.

Redeem

If someone has given you a gift certificate, or if you have a prepaid iTunes card, this page is where you cash it in. Click the Redeem link, and you'll be taken to the Redeem Code screen, where you enter the card's code and click Redeem to obtain credits for whatever the card promises. The amount of the card is added to your iTunes account and appears to the left of your Apple ID in the navigation bar.

Buy iTunes Gifts

Just like a real store, the iTunes Store lets you purchase and redeem gift certificates. It also lets you create a monthly iTunes Store allowance for that someone special. Click this link to be taken to a page where you can do this and more (**Figure 5.10**).

Figure 5.10
Some of The Store's gift options.

The page works this way.

Email Gift Certificates

Click this link to be taken to a page where you can send someone an iTunes gift certificate via email in amounts ranging from $10 to $200. Just fill in your name, the recipient's name, and the recipient's email address; type a personal message, if you like; click Continue; and confirm your Apple ID and password. Your gift is on its way.

Printable Gift Certificates

This option keeps you in The Store and produces a Printable Gift Certificates page. Fill in your name and the recipient's name, choose an amount ($10 to $200), type a personal message, and click Continue to purchase a gift certificate that you can print out and give to your dearest and possibly nearest.

Give Specific Music, TV Shows, and Movies

If you've ever listened to an album and thought, "My little snookums would love this!", here's your chance to do something about it. This option lets you give exactly the music, TV show, or movie you want.

Allowances

An iTunes allowance can best be described as a gift certificate that keeps on giving. After you create an allowance, the recipient of your largesse will have his or her Store credit bumped up by the amount that you've designated (values include $10 to $100 in $10 increments, $150, and $200) on the first day of each month. Just as when you purchase a gift certificate, your credit card will be charged, not the recipient's.

After you've created an allowance, a new Manage Allowances button appears on your Apple Account Information page. When you click this button, you go to the Edit Allowances page, where you can add allowances or suspend or revoke any that you've created. When you revoke an allowance, any balance placed in the account remains; it won't be credited back to you.

If you think you're going to reinstate that allowance later—when your daughter starts making her bed again, for example—click the Suspend button. (If you click Remove, you won't be able to put that allowance back into service; you must create a new one.) To reactive a suspended account, return to this screen and click the Activate button next to the account name. When you do, a dialog box appears, asking whether you'd like to send the allowance immediately or wait until the first of the next month.

tip If you tend to spend too much at The Store, you can create an allowance for yourself, but you can't do it simply by signing up for one. The Store prevents you from purchasing an allowance for the same Apple ID that receives the allowance. Instead, you must create a second Apple ID. (You'll need a different email address for this account, but you can use the same credit card that you use for your original account.) Sign on with that second ID and then purchase an allowance for your original account.

iTunes Gift Cards

Click this link, and your Web browser takes you to the online Apple Store, where you can purchase iTunes gift certificates.

Power Search

If you want to be a power shopper, you must learn to take advantage of The Store's Power Search function.

When you click the Power Search link on the main page, you're taken to a page where you can get very specific with your search. You'll see a Power Search pop-up menu that includes All Results, Music, Movies, TV Shows, Applications, Audiobooks, Podcasts, and iTunes U entries. Click the appropriate entry, and the fields below change to reflect search criteria. Choose the Music entry, and you can enter information in the Artist, Composer, Song, and Album fields, as well as choose a genre from the Genre pop-up menu. Click Movies, and you can search for Movie Title, Actor, Director/Producer, Year, Description, Genre, and Rating (All Ratings, G, PG, PG-13, or R).

tip **Many of the entries carry helpful options specific to the medium in question. When you choose Movies, for example, you get options to search for movies available for rent as well as for movies that offer closed captioning. You can also search podcasts for just video podcasts or search TV shows for only those series offered in HD.**

Browse

The Store offers a view much like the one you see in iTunes when you select a library entry or a playlist and choose View > Show Column Browser. (In point of fact, choosing this command produces the same result as clicking the Browse link.) Click Browse, and iTunes' browser columns appear:

- **App Store.** Again, I'll leave this topic for the iPod touch and iPhone books.

- **Audiobooks.** Choose Audiobooks, and the next column adopts a Genre heading with various literary genres below (such as Classics, Kids & Young Adults, and Mystery). Choose a genre, and authors/narrators writing or speaking in that style appear in the Author/Narrator column to the right. Select an author or narrator, and a list of that person's available work appears at the bottom of the window.

- **Movies.** Select Movies, and a list of genres appears to the right— Action & Adventure, Comedy, and Thriller, for example. Select one of these categories to see a list of movies that match.

- **Music.** Clicking Music produces four additional columns: Genre, Subgenre, Artist, and Album. You know what to do.

- **Music Videos.** Music Videos are broken into genres as well—Alternative, Blues, Holiday, Jazz, and Soundtrack, for example. Select a genre, and a list of appropriate artists appears to the right. Click an artist to see what he's or she's been up to in front of the cameras.

- **Podcasts.** To the right of this entry, you see Category and Subcategory columns. Choose Technology and then Tech News, for example, and a list of podcasts appears below. (There are so many technology podcasts, and this area is so disorganized, that it helps to know what you're looking for.)

■ **TV Shows.** TV Shows is broken down by Genre (including All HD for those times when you seek the best-looking episodes at The Store), TV Shows (24, *The Daily Show with Jon Stewart, Flight of the Conchords,* and *Weeds,* for example), and Season. Select a TV series, and (if offered) a list of seasons appears to the right. Choose a season to view individual episodes below (**Figure 5.11**). (If the series doesn't have multiple seasons, just clicking the name of the show will produce the list of available episodes at the bottom of the window.)

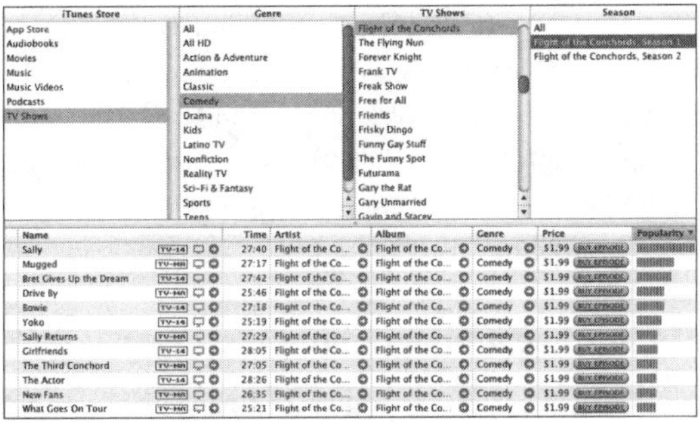

Figure 5.11

Browsing The Store's TV Shows.

The results area is divided into columns titled Name, Time, Artist, Album, Genre, Price, and Popularity, regardless of whether you're looking at music, movies, music videos, or TV shows. You can sort the list by any of these criteria by clicking the appropriate column head. Click Artist, for example, and the list is sorted alphabetically by artist. Click Time, and the list is sorted by shortest to longest playing time.

tip You'll notice a right-pointing arrow to the right of entries in some of these views. Clicking this arrow allows you to travel to the page devoted to that item—a great way to explore an album or an artist's catalog after searching for a single song, for example.

Account

Care to view or edit the information Apple has about you and your credit card? Wonder how you've spent your money at The Store? Want to cancel a movie you've preordered? You can do it all here. When you click the Account link, you'll be asked for your iTunes password. (You can also move to your Apple Account Information page by clicking your account name at the top of the iTunes window.)

Support

With this book at your side (or, better yet, open in front of your face), you shouldn't need to click The Store's Support link, but should you come across a problem that's arisen since the publication of this edition, click this link to open your Web browser and be taken to Apple's iTunes Store Support page. Here, you'll find answers to frequently asked questions about both iTunes and The Store, as well as customer service, billing, and troubleshooting links.

Genius Recommendations

You've been here before. Again, this page displays items that The Store believes you'll enjoy.

My Wish List

At one time, The Store offered a feature called Shopping Cart. Instead of using the typical "click and buy" approach to shopping, you could click an Add button that would add items to this Shopping Cart holding area. When you were ready to check out, you'd move to Shopping Cart, take another glance at the accumulated items, decide whether you *really* needed to spend that kind of money, and then buy everything in the cart at one go.

With iTunes 9, Shopping Cart is history, replaced by My Wish List. It works similarly, but unlike Shopping Cart, it doesn't require you to muck with iTunes' preferences. To use it, simply click the down-pointing triangle next to something that you're thinking about purchasing, and choose Add to Wish List. (This feature works only for purchases, not for movie rentals.) Add to Wish List is The Store's command, and the item will indeed be placed where you asked.

The Wish List entry on the home page will note the number of items in your Wish List. Move to the Wish List page by clicking the same-named link, and all the items you've added will appear (**Figure 5.12**). You can purchase them separately by clicking the Buy button next to each item or purchase everything in the Wish List by clicking the Buy All button at the top of the window. To remove items from the Wish List, just hover your cursor over them and click the small X in the top-left corner of the item (much as you'd click a window's Close box). *Poof*, it's gone.

Figure 5.12
I wish I could afford everything in my Wish List.

My Alerts

If you'd like to stay up to date on the releases of favorite artists, you can do so by clicking the Alert Me link in the Quick Links section of an artist's page. When you do, you can elect to receive email from Apple whenever that artist has released something new. Additionally, when you click the My Alerts link on The Store's home page, you're taken to a page that lists recent releases by artists whose work you've purchased from The Store.

Complete My Album

If you purchase a couple of tracks from an album and later decide that you'd like to have the entire album, the Complete My Album feature allows you to do so without having to repurchase those tracks. Click this link, and you see a list of albums of which you've purchased portions. Next to each album is what it will cost to complete the album—*Complete My Album for $8.70,* for example.

iTunes Plus

Up until mid-2007, the iTunes Store offered music that was copy-protected with Apple's FairPlay digital rights management (DRM) technology. FairPlay limits you to playing your purchased music on five computers. In mid-2007, Apple unveiled iTunes Plus—unprotected music tracks in AAC format encoded at high bit rates (256 Kbps) and sold initially for $1.29 per track, versus 99 cents for protected music tracks. In October 2007, Apple reduced the price of iTunes Plus tracks to 99 cents each (the single track price at the time).

When you click the iTunes Plus link, the iTunes Plus page appears. At the top of the pane is the Buy All button. Next to this button, you see the total number of tracks in your purchased library that you can update, along with the number of single tracks, albums, and music videos (**Figure 5.13**). Below this area is a list of albums that you can upgrade. At the bottom of the window is a list of upgradable tracks. Song upgrades are 30 cents each, album upgrades are 30 percent of the album's current sale price, and music videos cost 60 cents each to upgrade. At one time, you couldn't upgrade individual items; it was all or nothing. Now you're welcome to pick exactly the items you'd like to upgrade.

Figure 5.13

You can upgrade your protected purchased iTunes music to an unprotected, higher-bit-rate form.

Get the Goods

Now that you have an account and can find your way around The Store, it's time to stop manhandling the merchandise and actually buy something. You'll be amazed by how easy (and addictive) this can be.

Typical shopping at The Store is akin to going to a record store, picking up a CD, taking it to the counter, purchasing the disc, returning to the store to pick another CD, purchasing it, going back to the store once again, and ... well, you get the idea. You pay as you go. This is how the iTunes Store operates by default:

1. Pick your Poison (or Prince, *Prison Break,* or *Pirates of the Caribbean*).

    Using any of the methods I suggest earlier, locate music, audiobooks, or video that you desperately need to own.

2. Click the Buy button.

    To purchase a song or TV episode, click the Buy Song or Buy Episode entry in the Price column that appears in iTunes' main window.

To purchase an album, TV season, movie, or audiobook, look near the top of the window for a Buy button. The price of your purchase is listed next to each of these buttons.

note At times, you can't download an entire album. Instead, The Store may list a partial album—one from which you can purchase only individual songs. At other times, you can't buy certain music tracks individually; you must purchase the entire album.

3. Enter your Apple ID or AOL screen name and password in the resulting window.

4. Click the Buy button.

   Just to make sure you weren't kidding around when you clicked the Buy button, a new window asks you to confirm your intention to make your purchase. Should you care to banish this window forevermore, check the Don't Warn Me Again check box.

tip Be careful about enabling the Don't Warn Me Again option if you have others in the household who have access to your computer. My daughter is now musically aware, for example, and is extremely interested in starting her own music library. I prefer that she not do that on my nickel.

   If you've decided not to purchase the item, click Cancel and go on with your life.

5. Click the Buy button again.

   A Downloads entry appears below the Store heading in iTunes' Source list. Click this entry, and you can watch your media download to your computer. If you like, click the Pause button next to anything downloading. You can click the Resume button that appears in its place to take up the download where you left off. (You might do this to force something you want to listen to *right now* to download before other media.) You're charged for your purchases immediately.

By the Buy Button

With iTunes 9, the Buy button earned a little company in the form of a down-pointing triangle that, when clicked, produces a short menu of options (**Figure 5.14**).

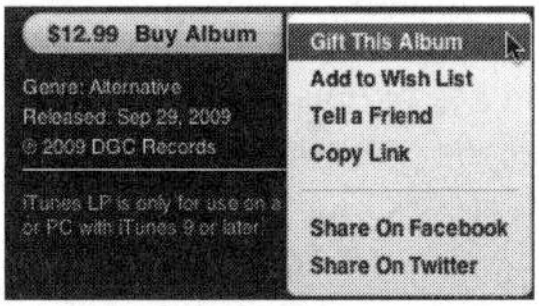

Figure 5.14
The Buy-button options.

Those options are

- **Gift This *X*** (where *X* is a song, album, movie, TV episode, or audio-book). Yep, the iTunes Store provides a way to purchase specific items and give them to your friends. Do this, and the recipient will get an email message (you must provide the address) with a link to the gift. When the giftee clicks this link, his or her default Web browser opens; then that computer's copy of iTunes opens to display the gifted item, which is ready to download.

- **Add to Wish List.** I cover Wish Lists earlier in this chapter.

- **Tell a Friend.** This option appears in menus associated with movies, TV shows, and albums, but not those for individual music tracks or audiobooks. Choose it, and a Tell a Friend pane appears, from which you can send an email message to one or more friends to promote that hunk of media.

- **Copy Link.** If you want to send someone a link to the item or publicize it on your blog, this option is how you obtain its address. When that link is clicked, the clicker's Web browser opens; then iTunes opens, and the linked page appears.

(continues on next page)

By the Buy Button (continued)

■ **Share On Facebook/Share On Twitter.** What better way to alert your friends and followers to the media you think worth their while? Choose Share On Facebook, and your Web browser opens; then a Facebook message is created that includes the item's title, artwork, and additional information that may include artist (music), director (movie), or episode (TV show). Choosing Share On Twitter takes you to your Twitter home page and composes a message with the item's title, a link, an iTunes hash tag (#itunes), and the kind of additional information sent with a Facebook message. If your browser won't log you into these services automatically, you'll be prompted for your user name and password.

Play with Your Purchase

After purchased media has found a home on your hard drive, you have several ways to put it to work.

Play it

You're allowed to play unprotected iTunes Plus music on as many computers, iPods, iPhones, and compatible music players as you like. The whole point of removing the protection was to give you this kind of freedom.

If you have older protected music purchased from the iTunes Store, you can play it on up to five computers. Purchased movies, TV shows, and audiobooks can be played only on computers authorized with your iTunes account. (You can also play these movies and TV shows on Apple's set-top media player, Apple TV.) When you play purchased media for the first time, iTunes checks to see whether the computer is authorized to play it. If so, the music, movie, audiobook, or TV show plays back with no problem. If the computer hasn't been authorized, you'll be prompted for your Apple ID or AOL screen name and password. That name and password, along with some information that identifies your computer, are sent to Apple, where that Mac or PC is counted against your limit of five authorizations.

If you've used up your authorizations on five other computers, you'll be notified that you must deauthorize one of your computers before you're allowed to play the purchased music. Fortunately, deauthorizing a computer is as simple as choosing Store > Deauthorize Computer. When you choose this command, your computer connects to the Internet, and Apple's database is updated to reflect the deauthorization of that particular computer.

tip **You say you've used up all your authorizations and can't remember exactly which computers you've authorized? No worries. Just start over. You can do that by accessing your Apple Account Information page, taking a gander at the Computer Authorizations entry, and clicking the Deauthorize All button. Doing so will do exactly what the button says and remove the authorization from every computer that had one. Note that this button won't appear until you've authorized five computers and that you can do this only once a year.**

After you deauthorize a computer, of course, you can't use it to play back purchased media until you authorize it again. (Yes, this means that if you own more than five computers and intend to play purchased media on all of them, you're going to spend some time playing the deauthorization shuffle.)

 Reformatting the computer's hard drive (or replacing that hard drive) doesn't deauthorize the machine. Before passing your computer along to someone else, be sure to deauthorize it.

Burn it

People play music on all kinds of devices and in all kinds of environments—on computers, boom boxes, home stereos, and portable music players, and in cars, boats, and planes. (I've even seen a system that allows you to play music in your hot tub.) Apple made this easier by stripping protection from its music, but not all music players support the AAC audio format that iTunes music is encoded with. Fortunately, iTunes allows you to burn your iTunes music to good old audio CDs.

When you do so, the music files are converted to Red Book audio files— the file format used by commercial audio CDs. These CDs are not copy-protected in any way and behave just like regular ol' audio CDs. Pop 'em into a standard CD player and press Play, and out comes the music.

There's no limit on how many tracks of unprotected music you can burn to CDs, but that older protected content does have some limitations. You can burn up to seven copies of a particular playlist that contains protected music, for example. If you attempt to burn an eighth copy, you'll be told that you can't. If you alter that playlist after the seventh burn—by adding or removing a song—you can burn another seven copies. Alter that playlist, and you get seven more copies.

To burn media to disc, create a playlist that contains the media you'd like to record to the disc. At the bottom of the playlist, you'll see a Burn Disc button. Insert a blank CD or DVD, and click this button to burn the contents of the playlist onto the disc.

If the playlist contains music only, you'll burn an audio CD. If you're attempting to burn video, that's a different story. iTunes doesn't allow you to burn video—TV shows, music videos, and movies—to discs that can be played in commercial players (such as the DVD player in your living room). Instead, iTunes lets you burn video only as data for purposes of backup.

Rent Movies

Early in 2008, Apple began offering movies for rent from the iTunes Store. These movies play not only on your computer, but also on iPods, iPhones, and Apple TV. Moving movies from iTunes to your iPod is different from the procedure for moving "regular" movies. It works like so:

1. Find a movie you want to rent at the iTunes Store.

   You can find movies by clicking Movies in The Store's navigation bar. In the resulting page, you'll see links to top movie rentals, along with thumbnail images of other movies you can rent. Click a thumbnail, and the movie page appears. Rentals cost $3 for older titles and $4 for new titles.

   > **note** After you rent a movie, you have 30 days to watch it before it's automatically deleted from your iTunes Library or from the device on which it currently resides. When you start watching a rental movie, you must finish watching it within 24 hours. Within that 24-hour period, however, you can watch it as many times as you like.

2. Click the Rent Movie button.

   The movie downloads to your computer and appears in the Rented Movie area, which you access by clicking Rented Movies in iTunes' Source list.

3. Move the rented movie to your iPod.

   Select your iPod in the Devices area of iTunes' Source list, and click the Movies tab. (Again, if your iPod can't play videos, no Movies tab appears, and you'll have to watch that rental on your computer or Apple TV.) At the top of this screen, you'll see the Rented Movies area. Below it are any unexpired movies that you've rented (**Figure 5.15** on the next page). Click the right-pointing Move arrow next to the movies you want to move to your iPod. The Sync button at the bottom of the iTunes window will change to Apply. Click Apply, and the button changes back to Sync. Click Sync, and the movie will be copied to the iPod.

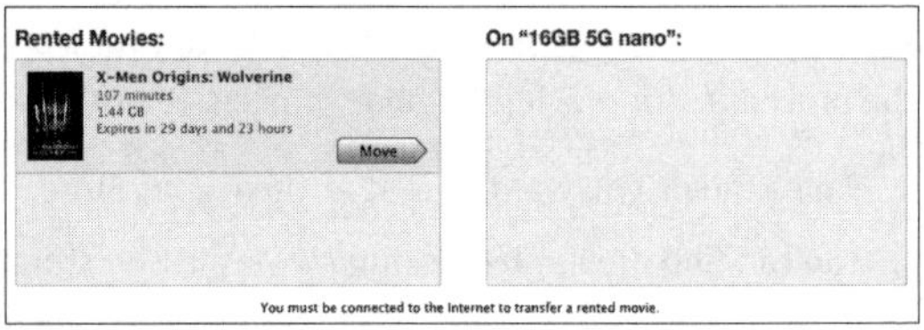

Figure 5.15

A rented movie, ready for transfer to an iPod nano.

Rented Movies:	On "16GB 5G nano":
X-Men Origins: Wolverine 107 minutes 1.44 GB Expires in 29 days and 23 hours Move	

You must be connected to the Internet to transfer a rented movie.

4. Watch the movie.

   After your rented movies are on the iPod, you can find them by name along with the other movies on your iPod.

5. Move the movie back to your computer, if you like.

   When you finish watching the movie, you may want to move it back to your computer so that you can watch it on that computer or move it to another compatible device that's registered with your iTunes account (a video-capable iPod, an iPhone, or Apple TV).

   To do this, mount the iPod, select it in iTunes' Source list, click the Movies tab, and in On *nameofipod* (which will be the name of your iPod), click the now-left-pointing Move arrow to return the movie to your iTunes Library.

6

The Informational iPod

By now, you probably realize that the iPod is the world's greatest porta-ble music player (and a pretty fair video player too!). But take a quick scroll through the Extras screen of a click-wheel iPod, and you'll get the idea that the iPod is more than a music player. On such an iPod, you'll find the Contacts, Calendars, and Notes entries, which hint that your iPod is ready to offer up a phone number, remind you of an upcoming appointment, or recall your Aunt Vilma's recipe for Swedish meatballs. In these pages, I show you how to take best advantage of these features by composing, moving, and synchronizing your contacts, calendars, and notes with your iPod.

Make iContact

There undoubtedly will come a time when a long-forgotten song that shuffles its way around your iPod reminds you of a friend, family member, or deadbeat client, and when that time comes, it may occur to you to get in touch with that person. An iPod packed with contacts can help in these moments. Here's how to make sure that those contacts and your iPod see eye to eye.

Viva vCard

To understand how the iPod works its contact magic, it's helpful to know that, like your computer, the iPod supports something called the *vCard standard*. This standard, concocted a couple of decades ago, allows you to read contact files created on a variety of devices—a computer, mobile phone, or personal information manager device, for example. The idea is that I can create a contact with my Mac's copy of Address Book and email it to my sister, who uses a Windows PC, and she can view that contact in her copy of Microsoft Outlook.

The iPod—clever little device that it is—supports vCards. Just plunk that vCard into the right folder on your iPod or sync it to your iPod with iTunes, and when you next click your iPod's Contacts entry, the rich details on that person, place, or thing will be revealed.

A vCard can display the following items:

- **Contact's picture.** Available on the 5G iPod, iPod classics, and 3–5G iPod nanos only.

- **Contact's formatted name.** Bubba Jones, for example.

- **Contact's name.** The name as it appears in the contact (Jones, Bubba, Dr., for example).

- **Contact's address(es).** The address types supported by vCard (business, home, mailing, and parcel).

- **Contact's telephone number(s).** The phone numbers supported by vCard.

- **Contact's email.** The email addresses in the contact.

- **Contact's title.** Dr., Ms., Mr., and so on.

- **Contact's organization.** The company name displayed in the contact.

- **Contact's URL.** The Internet address contained in the contact.

- **Contact's note.** The note field in the contact.

vCard support wouldn't mean much if common applications didn't support it. Fortunately, the universal nature of the standard means that most information-management and email applications you're likely to run across support vCard. Mac OS X's Address Book certainly supports it, as do Microsoft Entourage (Mac), Microsoft Outlook (Windows), Windows Address Book (XP), and Windows Contacts (Vista and Windows 7).

Syncing contacts to your iPod

All iPods save the shuffle can display contacts. To place contacts on your iPod, follow the steps for your operating system in the following sections.

Macintosh

Once upon a time, a program called iSync was responsible for syncing contacts and calendars with an iPod. No longer. Now iTunes offers this feature. Here's how it works:

1. Plug your iPod into your Mac.

2. Select your iPod in iTunes' Source list, and click the Contacts tab.

3. Enable the Sync Address Book Contacts option.

To place all the contacts in Address Book on your iPod, make sure that the All Contacts option is enabled. If you'd rather place only certain contacts on the iPod, enable the Selected Groups option, and in the list below, select the groups whose contacts you'd like to copy to the iPod (**Figure 6.1**). You may want only your business contacts or friends and family contacts on your iPod, for example. Grouping those contacts in Address Book and then selecting those groups in iTunes is the way to do it.

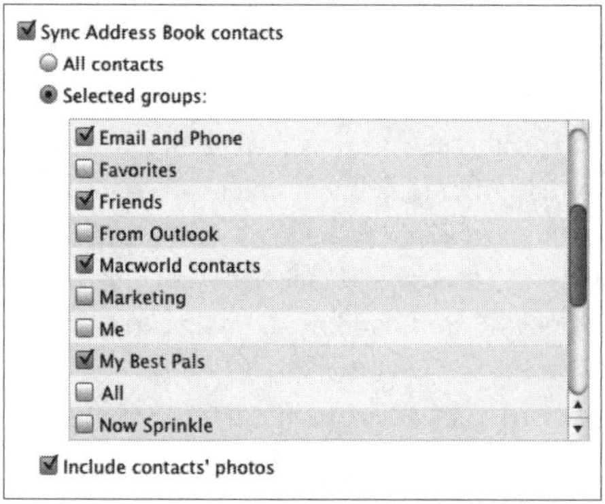

Figure 6.1

Selecting groups of contacts in iTunes.

☑ Sync Address Book contacts
  ○ All contacts
  ◉ Selected groups:

    ☑ Email and Phone
    ☐ Favorites
    ☑ Friends
    ☐ From Outlook
    ☑ Macworld contacts
    ☐ Marketing
    ☐ Me
    ☑ My Best Pals
    ☐ All
    ☐ Now Sprinkle

☑ Include contacts' photos

If you plug a 5G iPod, 3G–5G iPod nano, or iPod classic into your Mac, you'll see an option to copy your contacts' photos to the iPod. On a compatible iPod nano, these pictures will appear next to the contact's name as well as on the screen devoted to that contact. On a 5G iPod or iPod classic, the pictures appear only on the contact's screen.

4. Click the Apply button at the bottom of the pane.

iTunes synchronizes the selected contacts between your Mac and the iPod.

Windows

Fire up iTunes with your iPod connected, select your iPod in iTunes' Source list, and click the Contacts tab. Within this pane, you can elect to synchronize contacts from Windows Address Book (XP), Windows Contacts (Vista and Windows 7), or Microsoft Outlook. If you choose Outlook, you can synchronize all contacts or just selected groups. When you choose Outlook, by the way, it launches automatically.

The Manual Method

You have one additional way to put contacts on a click-wheel iPod:

1. Open your computer's Address Book application, and export your contacts as vCards.

2. Select the iPod in iTunes' Source list, click the Summary tab, and enable the Enable Disk Use option.

   This option mounts the iPod as if though were an external hard drive (which, indeed, it is).

3. Open the iPod "drive," locate the Contacts folder, and drag into this folder the vCards you exported earlier.

4. Unmount your iPod.

   The contacts will appear just as though you'd synced them via iTunes.

Managing contacts on click-wheel iPods

Contacts on iPod classics and the 4G and 5G iPod nanos are not presented in the same way. Although you find contacts in each model by choosing Extras in the Home screen, selecting Contacts, and pressing the Center button, you'll notice a stark difference after you press Center:

- On an iPod classic, all contacts are presented in a list, even if you've chosen to sync just certain groups of contacts. This means that if you have 2,500 contacts, you can expect your scrolling finger to get a workout, as you'll have to scroll through this long list to find the contact you want.

- The 4G and 5G iPod nanos, on the other hand, respect any groups that you've created in your computer's address-book application. When you select Contacts and press the Center button on one of these nanos, a Contact Group screen appears, listing all the groups you synced with the iPod. Simply select the group you want, press the Center button, and scroll to the contact.

On any of these iPods, to see full contact information, select the contact and press the Center button. You can move to the next or previous contact by pressing the Next or Previous button, respectively.

Sorting Your Contacts

I mention this topic in Chapter 2, but here's a gentle reminder: The iPod is just the tiniest bit flexible in how it lets you view your contacts, allowing you to sort them by first or last name.

To set your contact sorting preferences on a 4G or 5G iPod nano, choose Settings > General; scroll down to Sort Contacts; and press the Center button to toggle between Last and First (name) sorting.

The iPod classics work almost exactly the same way; the only difference is that their sort command is called Sort By and is located in the Settings screen.

Make a Date

As I explain earlier in the chapter, contacts and the iPod carry on their cozy relationship thanks to the vCard standard. Another couple of standards, called *vCal* and *iCalendar,* help the iPod understand calendar events. These standards are universal formats for exchanging calendar and scheduling information between vCal- and iCalendar-aware applications and devices.

When you add a calendar event to your iPod, the following information appears in the Event screen:

- **Date of the appointment.** Displayed in day/month/year format (11 Jan 2010, for example).

- **Time and duration of the appointment.** Displayed as 4:00–5:30 PM, for example.

- **Name of the appointment.** If you've named it My Appointment in your computer's calendar application, so shall it be named on your iPod.

- **Attendees.** If you've added attendees to the appointment in your computer's calendar application, those names will appear next in the Event screen.

- **Notes.** Any notes you've entered on your computer will appear last in the Event screen.

Working with calendars

Apple would have looked mighty foolish adding calendaring capabilities to the iPod without also providing Mac users a calendar application. It did so by releasing iCal, a free basic calendar application that runs under Mac OS X 10.2 and later.

iCal isn't the only Macintosh application that's compatible with the iPod, however. All of today's modern calendar applications can also export iPod-compatible calendar files (files saved in the vCal format).

Windows users can create iPod-friendly calendar files, too; unfortunately, they can't do it with an Apple application. Windows users who have a copy of Microsoft Office will discover that Outlook can export calendar files that are compatible with the iPod, as can other calendar applications that support the vCal format.

Syncing events on click-wheel iPods

The following sections show you how to make the most of the Calendars feature with your computer's common calendar applications and a click-wheel iPod.

iCal (Mac OS X)

Although you can move iCal calendars to your click-wheel iPod by selecting a calendar in iCal, choosing File > Export, and dragging the resulting calendar file into the iPod's Calendars folder, why bother when iTunes provides a more expedient method? To use iTunes, just follow these steps:

1. Plug your iPod into your Mac.

2. Select your iPod, and click the Contacts tab.

3. Enable the Sync iCal Calendars option.

   This procedure is sounding familiar, right? Yes, it's very much like moving contacts via iTunes. Similarly, you can choose to synchronize All Calendars or Selected Calendars. When you choose the latter option, just check the boxes next to the calendars you want to copy to the iPod (**Figure 6.2**).

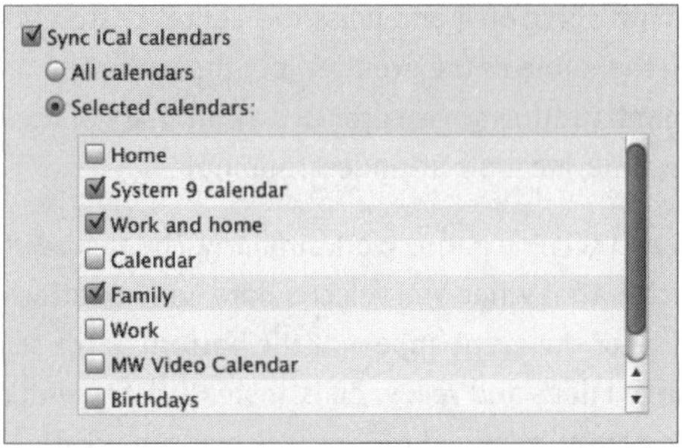

Figure 6.2

Selecting specific calendar entries.

4. Click the Apply button.

   iTunes synchronizes the selected calendars between your Mac and the iPod.

Outlook (Windows)

You guessed it—syncing calendars on a Windows PC is darned similar to doing it on the Mac. The major difference is that there is no iCal for Windows. Instead, you have the option to synchronize all your Outlook calendars or just selected calendars.

Viewing events on click-wheel iPods

The iPod classics and recent iPod nanos display events in nearly the same way. Just travel from the Home screen to Extras, select Calendars, and press the Center button. In the next screen, you'll see an All Calendars entry, followed by any separate calendars that you've synced to the iPod—Home and Work, for example. Select a calendar and press the Center button to display the current month's calendar.

On an iPod classic or a 3G iPod nano, days that hold events display a red flag, and those with alarms show a small yellow bell. When you select a date with a flag on it and press the Center button, you see a screen bearing the name of the event. Select the event and press the Center button; yet another screen provides a summary of the event, along with its date, time, location, attendees, and notes.

The 4G and 5G iPod nanos work similarly. The main difference in their approach is that when you select a date with an attached event, the time and name of the event appear at the bottom of the screen. These iPods lack the red flags and yellow bells. Instead, dates with events (with or without alarms attached to them) display a black dot.

To view the details of an event, select a date that has one and press the Center button, and that date's screen appears. Any events scheduled for that date appear in this screen, displaying the event's time and title. To move to the next day, press the Next button. To back up a day, press the Previous button. To get even more of an event's details, select the event and press the Center button. In the resulting screen, you see the event's title, date, and time, as well as any notes attached to it.

Notes-worthy Feature

Click-wheel iPods allow you to store small bits of text called Notes on them. Unlike their counterparts on an iPod touch or iPhone, however, these Notes are read-only; you can sync bits of text to the iPod and read them on the go, but you can't edit them.

If you select Notes in the Extras screen on a click-wheel iPod and then select the Instructions entry, you'll learn that you can view plain-text notes on your iPod. But there's more to know about Notes than that:

- **Notes are strictly limited to 4 Kbits.** If a note exceeds 4 Kbits (4,096 bytes), the excess text is cut off.

- **The iPod can hold up to 1,000 notes.** If the iPod's Notes folder contains more than 1,000 notes, only the first 1,000 are displayed. (The first 1,000 notes are determined by alphabetical order rather than creation date.)

- **Notes are cached in memory.** After you've viewed a note, its contents are stored in a 64 KB memory cache. This cache is useful because it allows the iPod to display the note without spinning up the hard drive on those iPods that have a hard drive, thereby extending the battery charge. When the cache overflows (because you've read more than 64 KB of data into it), the oldest notes are given the boot to make room for the information being copied into the cache.

- **Notes support a very basic set of HTML tags** (the Hypertext Markup Language codes used to create Web pages). These tags allow you to create notes that link to other notes or to media on your iPod. For more information on creating linked notes, see the iPod Notes Feature Guide (http://developer.apple.com/ipod/iPodNotesFeatureGuideCB.pdf).

Finally, you don't place notes on a click-wheel iPod through iTunes. Instead, mount the iPod on the desktop (you'll need to enable disk use for this to happen), double-click the iPod's icon to open it, and drag text files into the Notes folder. When you next access the Notes feature on the iPod, you'll find your notes within.

7

Accessories

At one time, nearly everything you needed for a happy iPodding experience came in the box: the iPod, a power adapter, the right cables, a case, a remote control, a Dock, and the software necessary to make it all work. That's changed—a lot. As Apple has lowered iPod prices while offering models with equal or higher capacities, it's determined to protect its profit by making once-bundled accessories pay-for options.

At the risk of verging onto the editorial, I don't think that's such a bad thing. Although I occasionally regret not getting a power adapter with each iPod, many people never use an adapter, as they routinely plug their iPods into their computers. And though it was nice enough to get a "free" case, the iPod case that was tossed into the box wasn't a particularly good one. If taking out the case knocks a few bucks off the price of an iPod, I'm more than happy to pay for a case that suits my needs.

Looking upon the dearth of accessories bundled with today's iPods as being an opportunity rather than a punishment, in this chapter I examine the kinds of items that will enhance your iPod.

Down to Cases

If you carry around an unprotected iPod classic or iPod nano, it won't be long before you notice the effect gravity can have on objects dropped from an inverted shirt pocket—or what a pants-pocketful of loose change and keys can do to an iPod's surface. Unless you like the distressed look, an iPod needs the protection that a good case can provide. And what will such a case provide?

What to look for

A good case should offer the following features:

- A system for attaching the iPod to your body (a belt clip or strap for the iPod; a case, lanyard, or clip for the iPod nano). The iPod shuffle has a clip built in, so you're set on that front.

- Construction sturdy enough to protect the iPod from scratches.

These features are the bare minimum you should expect from your case. Frankly, with a piece of bubble wrap, a clothespin, and a couple of pieces of duct tape, you could construct a case that meets these requirements. Looking beyond the essentials, what else might you look for?

- A way to detach the iPod from your body easily. At times, you'll want to fiddle with the iPod—adjust the volume, flick on the hold switch, or use the controls to skip a song. Look for a clip that releases quickly and effortlessly.

- A way to access the controls easily. An iPod classic or iPod nano case that opens in the front lets you fiddle with the controls. You should also be able to access the headphone jack—and, ideally, the Dock-connector port and hold switch—without having to disassemble the case. Also, if you often use the 5G iPod nano to shoot movies, you don't want a case that obscures the camera's lens.

- Design sturdy enough to provide your iPod a reasonable chance of survival, should you drop it.

- Design that makes a statement. Let's face it—you dropped a lot of cash on your iPod. The iPod is cool. It deserves a cool case.

On the cases

As this book goes to print, there are exactly 1 jillion iPod cases, and there's no way I can cover them all in this small book. Rather than recommend countless cases, I'll discuss the case styles you're likely to run across. Many case designs are available in different sizes (with variations in price) for full-size iPods and iPod nanos.

Hard-shell cases

Many iPod cases are designed primarily for protection. Oh, sure, they may be as fashionable as can be, but in addition to having a pretty face, each understands that its mission is to keep your iPod from exploding into a passel of parts should you drop it. The cases are generally made of polycarbonate plastic and, while surrounding the case, still provide access to the iPod's controls. DLO's $20 VideoShell (www.dlo.com) cases fill this bill.

Sports cases

Although you can subject hard-shell cases to a load of abuse, if you intend to expose your iPod to hostile environments—particularly those that are more than a little moist—seek a sports case. OtterBox (www.otterbox.com) has been making sturdy iPod and iPhone cases for a long time. Case names like Impact, Defender, and Armor assure you that the company has protection in mind for the active iPod owner (**Figure 7.1**).

Figure 7.1
*OtterBox's
Defender case for
iPod nano.*

COURTESY OF OTTERBOX.COM

Soft-shell cases

Despite the classification I've slapped on these things, soft-shell cases can also keep your iPod safe from harm. Marware's Sportsuit Convertible case (www.marware.com)—$35 for the classic and $30 for the iPod nano—is a good example of this kind of case (**Figure 7.2**). It provides coverage and opens so that you have access to the iPod's controls.

Figure 7.2
*Marware's
Sportsuit
Convertible case.*

COURTESY OF MARWARE

Skins and sleeves

At one time, skins really were skins—thin neoprene covers that protected the iPod from scratches but not bigger bumps. Although these skins are still around (and some of them look great), you can find tougher skins that provide more protection, such as Speck's $30 aptly named ToughSkin (www.speckproducts.com) for the iPod classic and the $20 PixelSkin for the 5G iPod nano.

Regardless of which display-bearing iPod you have, you might also look into the clear polymer films that protect the face and back of your iPod from scratches and smudges. These films are often included with cases. If the case you choose doesn't offer a film, take a look at Power Support's (www.powersupportusa.com) Crystal Film cover sets, for $15. You may feel a little put out about putting out that kind of money, but these films really do a good job of protecting the iPod.

Adaptive Technology

Although I've identified the small round hole at the top or bottom of the iPod as the headphone port, that port can accommodate more than just the iPod's earbuds. The iPod's headphone port can send out perfectly clean audio from this port to your computer's sound input port or to a home or car stereo. All you need to perform this feat is the right cable. I'll show you exactly which cables to use and how to string them properly from the iPod or Dock to the device of your choice.

iPod to computer

If you want to record directly from your iPod to your computer's audio port, you need an adapter cable that carries stereo Walkman-style 3.5mm miniplugs on both ends. (You can distinguish a stereo miniplug from the mono variety by the two black bands on the plug. A mono miniplug has just one black band.)

You can find such cables at your local electronics boutique for less than $5 for a 6-foot cable. Higher-quality cables that feature better shielding, thicker cable, and gold connectors can cost significantly more.

iPod to home stereo

Take the *personal* out of *personal music player* by attaching your iPod or Dock to your home stereo and subjecting the rest of the household to your musical whims. You need nothing more than a cable that features a stereo miniplug on one end and two mono RCA plugs on the other. A cheap version of this cable costs less than $5 (**Figure 7.3**).

Figure 7.3
Typical audio connectors (miniplug at top, RCA below).

Plug the miniplug into the iPod's or Dock's audio jack and the two RCA plugs into an input on your stereo receiver (the AUX input, for example). With this arrangement, you can control the volume not only with your stereo's volume control, but also (if the cable is connected to the head-phone port) with the iPod's scroll wheel.

iPod to two headphones

There may (and I hope there will) come a time when you'll want to snuggle up with your snookums and listen to your Special Song played on an iPod. A touch of romance goes out of this ritual, however, when you have to split a pair of earbuds between your li'l sweet potato and you.

To bring the intimacy back to your musical relationship, purchase a stereo line splitter. Such an adapter bears a single stereo male miniplug connector on one end (the end that you plug into the iPod) and two stereo female miniplug connectors on the other. Plug a pair of headphones into each female connector, and you're set. Griffin Technology (www. griffintechnology.com) makes SmartShare, a $15 headphone splitter with volume controls for each output.

 If you're seeking good-quality cables for a bargain price, check out MonoPrice.com. You'll never shop at RadioShack again.

iPod to car stereo

This one's a bit trickier. Increasingly, car stereos include an iPod Dock connector or miniplug jacks for plugging devices such as your iPod into the car's sound system. If you have such a connector or jack, you're in luck. Just use the appropriate cable, and you're ready to rock.

If you don't have a connector, a technician at a Ye Olde Auto Stereo Shoppe may be able to provide one by tapping into a hidden connector on the back of the car stereo. (That same technician will certainly be able to recommend an in-car iPod system that won't cost you an arm and a leg.)

 Because I can't stress this enough, allow me to spell it out in this tip: You will be So Much Happier with a direct connection than you will with the two alternatives I'm about to provide. You'll get better sound, and you'll have to futz with your iPod and the gear attached to it far less often.

Tip aside, if running through the rigmarole of taking your car to Y.O.A.S.S. sounds like a bother (or just too expensive), or if you're renting a car and don't have the option for a direct connection, you have two other options: a cassette-player adapter or an FM transmitter.

Cassette-player adapter

If your car still has a cassette player—you know, one of those tape-based thingies your parents told you about—you can use a cassette adapter. This thing looks exactly like an audio cassette, save for the thin cable that trails from the back edge. To use one of these adapters, shove it into your car's cassette player, plug its cable into your iPod, and press the Play buttons on both the iPod and the cassette player. Music should issue from your car's speakers.

These adapters cost less than $20. Note, however, that an adapter that works in one cassette player may not work in another. Make sure that you can return it for a refund in case your player exhibits an aversion to these doodads.

FM transmitter

These devices work like radio stations, broadcasting whatever is plugged into them to a nearby FM radio. FM transmitters work in a very limited range. Move them more than a dozen feet from the radio's antenna, and you'll pick up interference. For this reason, most are not ideal for use with a home stereo.

Their effectiveness in an automobile depends on how heavily populated the airwaves around you are and how sensitive your car's antenna is. A strong radio signal will overpower these devices, rendering them ineffective. If you live in an urban area with a plethora of active radio stations (or you plan to travel in one routinely), you may want to explore a hard-wired connection or a cassette adapter.

If you're interested in such a device, look for one that plugs into your car's power adapter (called the "cigarette lighter" by us old-timers). Such adapters not only provide power to your iPod (a good thing), but also tend to put out a stronger signal than those that operate off the iPod's battery (**Figure 7.4**).

Figure 7.4
DLO's TuneDock Micro FM transmitter.

COURTESY DLO

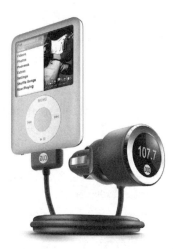

As the capabilities of FM transmitters change fairly frequently, I'll tell you only that these devices are made by companies such as Belkin (www.belkin. com), DLO, Griffin Technology, and Kensington (www.kensington.com).

Power to the People

Like the heads of government, your iPod needs power to do its job. To bring power to your iPod, consider these accessories.

iPod Power Adapter

Once upon a time, Apple included power adapters with full-size iPods. No more. Because it's a drag to have to find a computer with an available powered USB port (or FireWire port, if you have a very early iPod) to charge your iPod, I think that an iPod Power Adapter is a necessity. Apple will sell you one for $29.

If you have any other doodad that's powered from a USB power adapter—a pocket camcorder or an iPhone, for example—your iPod is compatible with that adapter too.

Griffin PowerDock

The iPod has been around long enough that some of us have more than one (personally, I've owned nearly 40 of the things). If you count yourself among the richly iPod endowed, one measly power adapter isn't going to cut it. To you, I recommend Griffin Technology's PowerDock, a charging base that includes either two ($40) or four ($70) slots (**Figure 7.5**). Just plug it in, insert the correct Dock adapter into each slot, and jack in your iPods and iPhones.

Figure 7.5
Griffin's four-slot PowerDock.

COURTESY GRIFFIN TECHNOLOGY

World Travel Adapter Kit

The iPod can automatically accommodate the world's two major power standards: 115 and 230 volts. The iPod Power Adapter, however, comes with just one plug—of whatever type is used in the country where it was sold. If you plan to take your iPod globetrotting, you'll need the proper plug adapter. Apple's $39 World Travel Adapter Kit contains plug adapters for outlets in North America, Japan, China, the United Kingdom, continental Europe, Korea, Australia, and Hong Kong.

Auto charger

To keep your iPod topped off on the road, you need an auto charger. The device plugs into your car's 12-volt receptacle and delivers power to your iPod through a plug that fits into the iPod's Dock-connector port. You'll find lots of these chargers on the market. Any number of companies make them, including Griffin Technology (PowerJolt) and DLO (Auto Charger).

Backup batteries

Fat lot of good a power adapter and auto charger do you if you're flying halfway around the world or traipsing through one of the less-welcoming Costa Rican jungles during the latest Eco-Challenge. If you plan to be removed from a ready source of power for a period longer than the typical life of an iPod charge, you need some extra help.

Currently, a variety of companies offer that help. I'm keen on the Richard Solo products (http://richardsolo.com). Prices range from $40 for the Backup Battery for iPhone/iPod to Dexim's $90 BluePack S3 2600 mAh for iPhone/iPod/BlackBerry (**Figure 7.6**).

Figure 7.6
*Dexim's BluePack
S3 battery pack.*

COURTESY RICHARDSOLO.COM

The Ears Have It

The iPod's earbuds are perfectly serviceable for most people; witness all the white earbuds in evidence on the street, in the subway, and up in the air. But this style of headphone is inherently problematic, because (a) not all ear canals are the same size, so a set of one-size-fits-all earbuds may not fit all, and (b) some people get the heebie-jeebies when items are lodged inside their ears. For these reasons, your list of accessories may include an additional set of headphones.

Headphones come in a variety of styles—including earbuds, neckband, open-air, and closed—from more companies than I can name. (I'll name a worthy few anyway: beyerdynamic, Etymotic Research, Future Sonics, Grado Labs, Koss, Sennheiser, Shure, Sony, and v-moda.)

Earbuds

If you like earbud-style headphones but find those included with the iPod to be uncomfortable, earbuds are available from a variety of manufacturers. Look for earbuds that fit well, don't require a lot of fiddling to focus (meaning that you don't have to move them around continually to make them sound good), and offer reasonably well-balanced sound.

Neckband headphones

These headphones, not as popular as they once were, are secured to your head with wires that drape over the tops of your ears. Imagine putting on a pair of tight glasses backward, so that the lenses are on the back of your head, and you'll get the idea. Neckband headphones are comfortable but easy to dislodge if you tug on the cable. Also, they don't provide a lot of sound isolation, which means that sounds from outside tend to filter through.

Open-air headphones

Open-air headphones sit over the ears without enclosing them completely. If you ever purchased a portable CD or DVD player, open-air headphones likely were included in the box. These headphones are comfortable, but the less-expensive models can sound thin. Like neck-band headphones, they don't provide much isolation.

Closed headphones

Closed headphones cover your ears completely and provide a lot of isolation, leaving you undistracted by outside sounds and those around you undisturbed by a lot of sound bleeding out of your headphones. Some closed headphones can be a bit bulky and uncomfortable, particularly if you wear glasses, so be sure to try before you buy. Also keep in mind that because of their size, these headphones aren't terribly portable.

Miscellanea

Then there are the iPod accessories that defy categorization. If you've done the rest, try these accessories on for size.

iPod microphones

At one time, full-size Dock-connector iPods could record "voice-quality" audio (8 kHz, mono) through a compatible microphone attachment. When Apple released the 5G iPod, it quietly included an unexpected upgrade; these new iPods can record CD-quality audio (44.1 kHz, stereo) with a compatible adapter.

Regrettably, the microphone adapters that plugged into the bottom of the iPod have largely disappeared. For the most part, that's fine for a couple of reasons. The first is that 4G and 5G iPod nanos and the 2G iPod classic can record audio through their headphone ports. If you have the headset that comes with the latest 32 GB or 64 GB iPod touch or an iPhone, you can record audio through its headset. Headset adapters that carry microphones, such as Griffin Technology's $20 SmartTalk, work too.

The second reason is that a good-quality mic still exists. Blue Microphones' $80 Mikey microphone (www.bluemic.com) plugs into the bottom of an iPod. It features three selectable gain settings (quiet, moderate, and loud) and is compatible with 2G–5G iPod nanos, the 5G iPod, and the iPod classics (**Figure 7.7**). It's a little bulky on smaller iPods, but the sound it records is good for a microphone of its size.

Figure 7.7
Blue Microphones'
Mikey iPod
microphone.

COURTESY OF BLUE MICROPHONES

Wireless transmitter

Suppose that you have an iPod in your hand, and you'd like its sound to come out of the powered speakers across the room. Normally, you'd attach it to those speakers with a Dock or audio cable . . . but you don't have to. Audioengine (www.audioengineusa.com) makes a little something called the $169 Audioengine W2 (**Figure 7.8**), a transmitter that you plug into the iPod's Dock connector. Then you plug the accompanying receiver into your powered speakers and play music as you normally would. The W2 transmits the iPod's audio to the receiver and speakers or amplifier it's plugged into. Kinda nifty.

Figure 7.8
Audioengine W2
wireless iPod
transmitter.
COURTESY OF AUDIOENGINE

AV Dock

As you know, recent Dock-connector iPods can play video on an attached TV via a compatible cable plugged into the Dock-connector port. You can manage this with one of Apple's $49 AV cables (which come in composite and component video flavors). These cables include an iPod power adapter so that you can charge your iPod as you watch its output on your TV. But if you add an AV dock, you have the option to not only power the iPod, but also control it from the comfort of the couch and navigate it via a remote control and interface that appears on the TV screen.

DLO offers two such docks: the $150 HomeDock Deluxe and the $200 HomeDock HD. The HomeDock Deluxe supports Composite video via S-Video and RCA connections. The HomeDock HD includes these same connectors as well as HDMI output—a high-definition connector used on most of today's HD TVs (**Figure 7.9**).

Figure 7.9
DLO's HomeDock
HD.
COURTESY OF DLO

note No iPod can play HD video. What the HomeDock HD does is upscale the iPod's standard-definition video to 720p or 1080p HD. It looks good, but it's not true HD.

Speakers

The best way to share your iPod's music with those around you is to jack it into a set of powered speakers. Thanks to the iPod's phenomenal popularity, you can find iPod-friendly speakers that fit just about every budget and taste.

Generally speaking, these speakers include some variety of Dock connector for plugging in your iPod—though many also include a miniplug input port that allows you to plug in older iPods that don't have Dock-connector ports, as well as other audio devices such as CD players.

iPod speaker systems come in a variety of sizes and suit different purposes. You can spend a lot of money on great powered speakers, complete with remote control, that rival or surpass your stereo gear (**Figure 7.10**). You can spend very little money and get a set of powered speakers that fits in a backpack or purse. And you can spend a moderate amount of money and get a great-sounding clock radio that also accommodates your iPod.

Figure 7.10
B&W's aptly-name Zeppelin speakers.

COURTESY OF B&W

At one time, I could have rattled off half a dozen good-sounding speaker systems that don't cost an arm and a leg, but there are so many of these things now, and speakers are such a personal choice, that I'll instead rattle off a few company names—Altec Lansing, Audioengine, B&W, Boston Acoustic, Bose, iHome, JBL, Logitech, and Tivoli Audio—and suggest that you visit your local sound store and listen to as many systems as you can stand.

8

Tips and Tricks

You're far enough along in this little guide to understand that the iPod and iTunes hold more secrets than just Rip, Click, and Play. This dynamic duo have other wonders to behold if you know how to unleash them. And that's exactly the point of this chapter: to shed light on the lesser-known marvels of the iPod and iTunes.

Let the magic begin.

Move Media off the iPod

To deter piracy, iTunes and the iPod were designed so that media would travel in one direction only: from the computer to the iPod. When you double-click an iPod mounted on a computer, you'll find no folder within that holds the device's music or movies. Yet this material has to be there somewhere.

It is. It's invisible.

When Apple designed the original iPod's copy-protection scheme, it understood one of the fundamental laws of this new millennium: That which can be locked will be unlocked (by a 12-year-old).

In past editions of this book, I revealed ways to make the iPod's Music folder visible and then copy files from this folder to your computer. Although this process is an interesting academic exercise, it's largely a waste of your time. Scan sites such as Download.com and VersionTracker (www.versiontracker.com), and you'll discover a host of utilities designed to pull media off your iPod and put it on your computer. Some of these utilities are more sophisticated than others, allowing you to copy not only the music the iPod carries, but its playlists as well. Here are a handful of my favorites.

Macintosh utilities

Sci-Fi Hi-Fi's $8 PodWorks (www.scifihifi.com/podworks) is the goods for Mac users (**Figure 8.1**). Because it reads the iPod's internal database rather than individual song data, it's fast. It can also sort tracks by the ID3 tags (see Chapter 4) contained in that internal database, making it easier to find just the tracks you want. It can copy entire playlists—as well as individual items—from the iPod in a single drag, and when it does, it maintains the original's play count, star ratings, and date-added information.

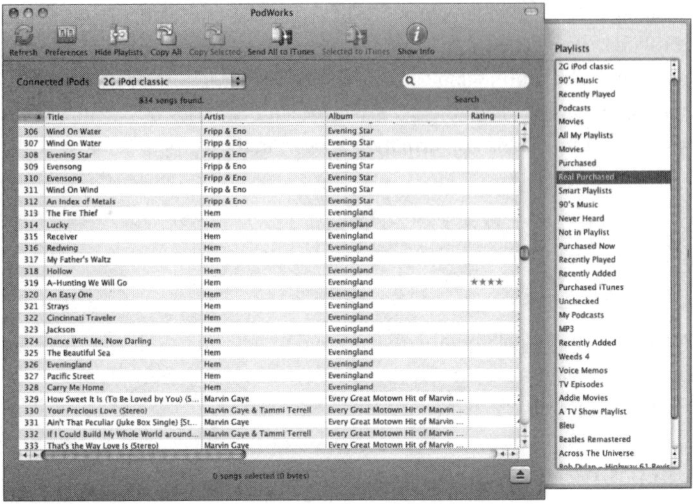

Figure 8.1 *PodWorks.*

Additionally, PodWorks lets you preview songs from the iPod—a helpful feature if you're not sure whether you're looking at the studio version or the live version of a particular cut.

Finally, you can run PodWorks directly from the iPod. This capability is useful for those rare occasions when you've lost your iTunes Library (and, thus, need this tool) because your entire hard drive has gone the way of the dodo and taken its copy of PodWorks with it.

Windows utilities

WindSolutions' $20 CopyTrans (www.copytrans.net) works with click-wheel iPods as well as the iPod touch and iPhone. Its capabilities match those of PodWorks. Also like PodWorks, it features an iPod-like interface and can copy music as well as video from the iPod to a Windows PC.

iPodSoft's $20 iGadget (www.ipodsoft.com) can also move media from the iPod to your PC (or Mac, as a version is available for that computing platform too), exporting movies, single songs, or playlists. In addition, it can transfer data such as weather forecasts, local movie times, driving directions, and RSS news feeds. This information appears in the iPod's Notes area.

Get the Greatest Charge out of Your iPod

No, I'm not being colloquial. I don't intend to tell you how to get the greatest thrill out of your iPod, but how to coax the longest play time from a single battery charge. Try these tips.

Keep it warm (but not too warm)

Lithium-ion polymer batteries perform at their best when they're operated at room temperature. If your iPod is cold, warm it up by putting it under your arm (which, with a really chilly iPod, is an invigorating way to wake up in the morning). And keep your iPod out of your car's hot glove compartment.

Use it at least once a month

I can't imagine owning an iPod that you never unplug from a power source, but it takes all kinds to make a world. The iPod's battery likes to have its little electrons banged around at least once a month. Do so by unplugging it and using it as Jobs intended.

Flip on the hold switch

If you accidentally turn on your traditional iPod while it's in a pocket, purse, or backpack, you'll be disappointed hours later when you discover

that its battery has been drained by playing only for itself. An engaged
hold switch will keep this from occurring.

Don't touch it

OK, that's a bit extreme. What I really mean is that every time you press
a button, the iPod has to make an additional effort, which drains the
battery faster.

Turn off the extras

Try shutting down EQ and Sound Check, and don't use backlighting.
These extras—particularly backlighting—eat into your battery's charge.

Load your iPod classic with smaller files

The more often your iPod classic's hard drive spins up, and its memory
cache fills and empties, the more quickly its battery is drained. Files that
exceed 9 MB force more frequent hard-drive spins and cache activity. For
this reason, you'll get more play time from your iPod classic if your song
files are in the compressed AAC and MP3 formats versus the big ol' AIFF,
WAV, and Apple Lossless formats.

Turn down the brightness control

All of today's screen-bearing iPods include brightness controls. The
brighter your iPod's display, the faster your battery drains.

Shift Your iTunes Library

It may not happen today, tomorrow, or next year, but if you're an iTunes
enthusiast, your computer's startup drive will eventually be so choked
with media that you won't have room for anything else. When this

happens, you'll want to move your iTunes Library to another hard drive. Here's how:

1. Create a new location for your media files (a folder on an additional internal or external hard drive, for example).

2. Launch iTunes, and choose iTunes > Preferences (Mac) or Edit > Preferences (Windows) to open the iTunes Preferences window.

3. Click the Advanced tab and then click the Change button.

   The Change Music Folder Location dialog box opens.

4. Navigate to the new location you created in step 1, and click Open.

5. In that same Advanced tab of the iTunes Preferences window, enable the options labeled Keep iTunes Media Folder Organized and Copy Files to iTunes Media Folder When Adding to Library; then click OK to dismiss the Preferences window.

6. Choose File > Library > Organize Library.

   In the Organize Library dialog box that appears, you see two options: Consolidate Files and Upgrade to iTunes Media Organization (**Figure 8.2**). Consolidate Files is the option you're interested in. Enable this option to copy all your media files to the iTunes Music folder that you've designated in the Advanced preference. The original files remain in their original locations, so when you're sure that your files have been copied where you want them, you may want to dispose of the originals.

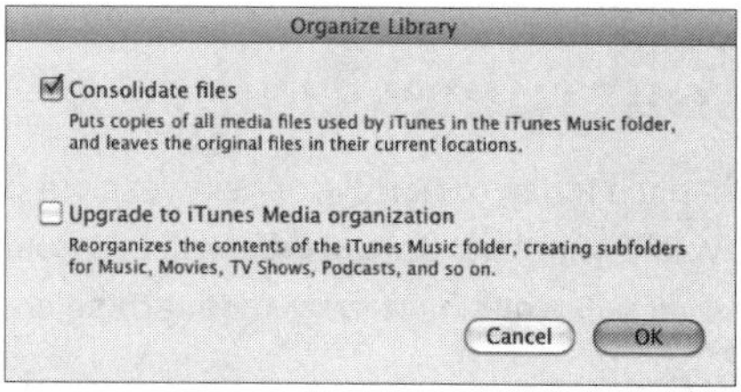

Figure 8.2

Select the Consolidate Files option in iTunes' Organize Library dialog box.

Organize Library

☑ Consolidate files
Puts copies of all media files used by iTunes in the iTunes Music folder, and leaves the original files in their current locations.

☐ Upgrade to iTunes Media organization
Reorganizes the contents of the iTunes Music folder, creating subfolders for Music, Movies, TV Shows, Podcasts, and so on.

Cancel   OK

7. Click OK.

   iTunes copies not only your files to the destination you designated, but also your library's playlists. (It maintains ratings as well.)

note With iTunes 7 and later, you can span an iTunes Library across volumes. To do this, open the Advanced tab of the iTunes Preferences window, click the Change button, and designate a new iTunes Music folder location. When you turn off the Copy Files to iTunes Music Folder When Adding to Library option, iTunes will look to this new folder while maintaining contact with the old one; you can play the files in your old iTunes Music folder as well as the files in the new folder. When you add new music, that music will be added to the new location.

Copy Media from Other Computers

It's quite common to have more than one computer in your home and nearly as common to have media libraries with different contents on each computer. In the past, moving media from one computer to another was inconvenient. No more. Apple has made this process easier, thanks to the new Home Sharing feature in iTunes 9. Here's how it works between two computers:

1. Open iTunes' Preferences window on each computer, and click the Sharing tab.

2. On the computer from which you want to copy media, enable the Share My Library on My Local Network option.

   If you like, you can share just selected playlists or your entire iTunes Library.

3. On the computer to which you want to copy media, enable the Look for Shared Libraries option.

4. On the computer that will receive the copies, go to iTunes' Source list (below the Shared heading), and select the computer you want to copy from.

5. Still on the destination computer, from the Show pop-up menu at the bottom of the iTunes window, choose Items Not in My Library (**Figure 8.3**).

Figure 8.3 *Copying music from one computer to another with iTunes' Home Sharing feature.*

You also have the option to show all items in the other library, but for this exercise, you're concerned about copying just the media you don't have.

6. Select the files that you'd like to copy from the other computer, and click the Import button at the bottom of the iTunes window.

The files will be copied to the computer's iTunes Library.

Home Sharing offers an additional benefit that you should be aware of: You can automatically transfer media that you purchase from the iTunes Store to another computer. Click the Settings button at the bottom of the iTunes window (again, with the shared computer selected), and a Home Sharing Settings dialog box appears. In this dialog box, you can designate the kinds of media to be transferred to this computer automatically when they're purchased on the other computer (**Figure 8.4**).

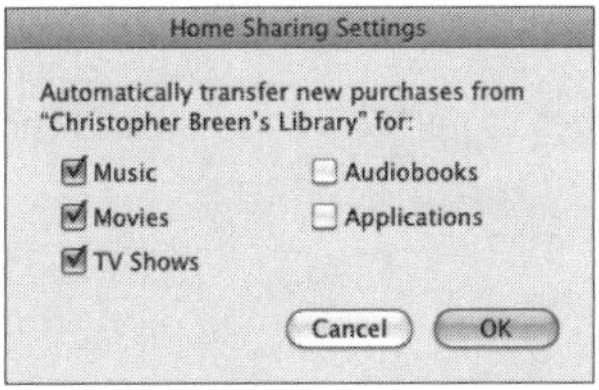

Figure 8.4
iTunes' Home Sharing screen.

Home Sharing Settings

Automatically transfer new purchases from "Christopher Breen's Library" for:

☑ Music   ☐ Audiobooks
☑ Movies   ☐ Applications
☑ TV Shows

(Cancel) (OK)

So, for example, if your husband just picked up Weezer's new album on his laptop, and if you enabled the Music option on your computer prior to that purchase, that album will be transferred to your computer automatically.

> **note** Before you can transfer purchased content from one computer to another, both computers must be authorized with the Apple ID used to purchase that content.

Rip Your DVDs

Here's a little scientific fact that may have missed your notice.

If you take a 5-year-old, wash him thoroughly, dress him in sterile garb, and put him inside a "clean room" along with your favorite DVD, he—and the DVD—will emerge 20 minutes later covered in jam *even though there's no jam within 50 miles of the facility!*

Yes, 5-year-olds have an unearthly power to channel jam (typically, strawberry) from the ether and smear it on your precious movie discs. And because they do, it's imperative that you find a way to back up those discs before they get smeared and you have to replace them with unjammed copies.

Also, given that you have an iPod, wouldn't it be cool if you could take the DVDs that you own and convert them so that they can be played on your iPod? Yes, it would—and yes, you can.

You have a variety of ways to perform this feat, as I show you in the following sections.

Macintosh

If you have a Mac, you're in luck; you can do this for free. Here's how:

1. Download and install a copy of the VideoLAN Client (VLC) from www.videolan.org.

   VLC contains components that help remove the copy protection from commercial DVDs.

2. Download and install a copy of HandBrake from http://handbrake.fr.

3. Slip a DVD into your Mac's media drive.

4. When you're prompted, select the DVD in the resulting sheet and then choose the disc's Video_TS folder.

   HandBrake scans the disc, seeking the main disc's main feature. The main title appears in the Title pop-up menu.

5. Choose your encoding preset.

   If the Presets pane doesn't appear, click the Toggle Presets button at the top of the window, and from the Presets pane, choose the device you'd like to watch the movie on—iPod, for example (**Figure 8.5**).

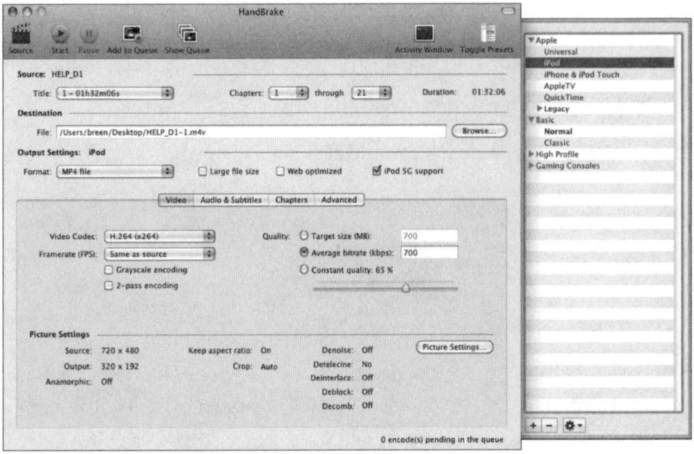

Figure 8.5 *HandBrake is a terrific (and free) tool for ripping DVDs on the Mac.*

6. Wait about an hour for HandBrake to rip your disc.

   When it's done, it automatically places a copy of the movie in your iTunes Library so that the movie is ready to sync to your iPod.

Or . . .

1. Download a copy of Metakine's Fairmount (which is free) from www. metakine.com/products/fairmount.

   Fairmount will mount the DVD as an unprotected disc.

2. Convert the disc with a third-party utility.

   We leave the land of the free at this point, I'm afraid. Utilities such as Roxio's $100 Toast Titanium (www.roxio.com) and the €40 DVD2one (www.dvd2one.com) can convert the now-unprotected DVD to a form that's playable on your iPod.

Or . . .

1. Purchase a copy of The Little App Factory's $20 RipIt (http://ripitapp.com). RipIt is the simplest of the Mac bunch.

2. Insert your disc, launch RipIt, and click the Rip button.

    In about an hour, an exact copy (without the copy protection) will be on your Mac. At that point, you can use HandBrake to convert it to a format that's compatible with your iPod.

Windows

Yes, there are tools for Windows users as well. The one that gets the bulk of the attention is SlySoft's AnyDVD (www.slysoft.com), which is sold on a subscription basis. You can use it for a year for €41, 2 years for €49, 3 years for €56, or 4 years for €61, and €64 gets you a lifetime subscription. You're welcome to give it a go for 21 days to see whether you like it. If so, go ahead and buy.

It works this way:

1. Launch AnyDVD, and insert a DVD.

2. Select Video DVD in the Status pane.

3. Enable the Remove Annoying Adverts and Trailers options.

    These options ensure that just the main feature will be ripped.

4. Click OK.

    AnyDVD rips the movie.

Wrangling the Legal and Moral Issues

Wait—isn't it illegal to rip DVDs? It's a gray area, because two conflicting laws are involved:

- **Fair Use.** The Fair Use component of U.S. copyright law says that under certain circumstances, it's OK to make backup copies of the media that you own.

- **DMCA.** The Digital Millennium Copyright Act (DMCA) states that you're in violation of this act if you defeat a copy-protection scheme.

So which is it? Only the courts can tell us, and so far, they've been loath to weigh in. What they *have* decided is that it appears to be against the law to manufacture tools that defeat copy protection, but it's okay to employ them for personal use. *Right.*

The problem for the copyright cops is that these tools are made and sold outside the United States, which places them outside the jurisdiction of the DMCA—which, therefore, is not a terribly effective bit of legislation.

Now let's talk briefly about morality. Forget the law; forget the courts; forget the media companies. Just know this: If you use these tools to rip DVDs that you don't own (and yes, I'm looking at you, Mr. and Mrs. Netflix subscriber), you will go to hell. Flaming, pitchfork-jabbing, sulfur-stinking, DVD-stealing, H-E-Double-Hockey-Sticks hell.

It's up to you to determine whether *The Wiggles Go Bananas!* is worth the price of your immortal soul.

Put Old Media on New iPods

Rummage around in the garage, attic, or wherever you keep your old junk, and you're sure to find at least one box that contains old VHS tapes, LPs, and cassettes. Word to the wise: This stuff isn't improving with age. Wouldn't it be nice if you could move some of that material to your computer and, thus, your iPod?

Of course you can. The process for doing this is called *digitizing* your media—converting it from its analog form to digital. Here's how to go about it.

VHS tapes

I hope that in addition to that box of VHS tapes, you still have your VHS player. These players aren't being made much anymore, so if you can't find yours, call your best packrat friend and borrow hers.

Using your camcorder

One method (a free one at that) for transferring VHS tapes to a computer is to use a camcorder as a go-between. Many camcorders have a *pass-through* mode that works like this:

1. String a cable between the video and audio outputs of the VHS player and the input ports of the camcorder.

   The VHS player likely has S-Video and composite video outputs and certainly will sport RCA audio jacks. Use S-Video if it's available, as it provides better-quality video.

2. Run a cable between the camcorder and your computer.

   This cable will be either FireWire or USB, depending on the kind of connection your camcorder supports for transferring video to a computer.

3. Read the camcorder's manual to find out how it handles pass-through.

   It may work without your having to do a thing, but some camcorders require you to enable a setting that allows video to pass through the camera.

4. Launch the video-capture software on your computer, and record the output of the VHS player.

   For the Mac, this software would be iMovie. For Windows, use Windows Movie Maker.

Buying an adapter

If you don't have a camcorder or one that supports pass-through, worry not; there's another way. That other way is simply to purchase a product intended for exactly this purpose.

For said purpose, I'd turn to Roxio, which offers two products for the job—one for Windows and another for the Mac. The Windows version, called Easy VHS to DVD, costs $60. The other version, Easy VHS to DVD for Mac, costs $80 (**Figure 8.6**). Why the $20 difference? The hardware is exactly the same, so let's just say that Mac users are known to have bits of extra cash sitting in their wallets.

Figure 8.6

Easy VHS to DVD for Mac can help you digitize your old VHS tapes.

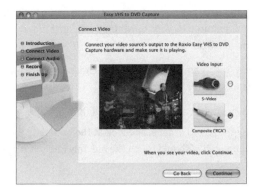

There's not much to using these tools. Just plug the USB capture device into a free USB 2.0 port on your computer, attach the proper cables (the capture device supports composite and S-Video as well as RCA audio), launch the software, and follow the steps. Each product walks you through the process. These devices allow you to encode video so that it plays natively on an iPod.

LPs and tapes

Like capturing and converting video, converting LPs and tapes is largely a matter of taking the output from the player (the turntable or cassette player), conveying it to the audio input of your computer, and then using software to capture and edit the sound.

After you've made the connection to your computer, the process is fairly simple. Like so:

1. If you don't have an audio-editing application, download a copy of Audacity (http://audacity.sourceforge.net).

   Audacity is a free, open-source audio recording and editing application that comes in versions for the Mac as well as Windows.

2. Launch Audacity, and choose an audio input.

   Open Audacity's Preferences, and in the Audio I/O preference, choose the input used by your turntable or cassette player. (This could be the Line-In port or a turntable's USB port, if you have a USB turntable.)

3. From the Channels pop-up menu, choose 2 (Stereo), and click OK to dismiss the Preferences window.

4. Play a sample, and adjust the input (if necessary).

   Play the record or tape, and look at the meters at the top of the window. They should touch the red only rarely. If they're in the red all the time, the sound will be distorted. If the green bars appear in only the first quarter of the meters, the sound will be too soft.

To adjust the input, use the slider with the Microphone icon next to it.

5. Click the Record button, and play the record or cassette.

The Record button is the round red button next to the green, triangular Play button.

That Dratted RIAA Curve

Records are recorded with something called the *RIAA curve*. When they're cut, low frequencies are reduced, and high frequencies are emphasized. When you play your records, special circuitry in your stereo receiver turns the tables, boosting low frequencies and reducing high frequencies. What this means for this particular bit of business is that if you plug a turntable directly into your computer, the resulting sound is going to be pretty awful. To get decent sound from your records into your computer, you must run the turntable through a preamplifier that deals with this curve.

Your stereo receiver has such a preamplifier. To get the proper sound from the record, you must channel the turntable through a receiver and then take the output from the receiver and plug it into your computer's audio input jack. (You'll likely need an RCA-to-stereo-miniplug adapter.)

Too complicated? Do you lack a turntable? No problem. LPs are making a comeback, and many new turntables include a USB cable that plugs directly into your computer. On your computer, the turntable is recognized as just another audio source. Several companies make these turntables, including ION Audio (www.ionaudio.com), Audio-Technica (www.audio-technica.com), Sony (www.sony.com), and Numark (www.numark.com). They start at less than $100.

6. Trim the audio.

   It's likely that you've captured a little more audio than you want. You can click and drag over the portion you don't want and then press the keyboard's Delete key to remove the detritus.

7. Split the audio.

   If you've recorded the side of an LP or cassette that includes multiple cuts, you'll want to split them into individual tracks. You can do this by clicking and dragging over the first track to select it and then choosing Edit > Split. This command cause a new track to appear below the first, containing the song you selected (**Figure 8.7**).

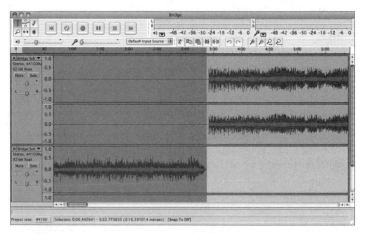

Figure 8.7 *Splitting audio tracks from a captured LP with Audacity.*

8. While that track is still selected, choose File > Export As WAV or File > Export As MP3, depending on whether you want an uncompressed or compressed version of the track.

9. Repeat this splitting-and-saving process (steps 7 and 8) for each track.

note I suggest Audacity because it's free and available for the computer you own, but lots of audio editors can do the job. Some will even detect the silence between tracks and then split and save the tracks for you.

Take Your iPod on the Road

Here are just a few of the travel tips I've picked up over the years.

No, it's not a flashlight, but . . .

I understand that a good way to run down an iPod's battery is to leave backlighting on all the time. I also understand that when you travel with a small child, and you leave the nightlight at home, you could be in for a lot of trouble from spouse and child.

I've had occasion to use an iPod as a nightlight under these very conditions. To ensure that the battery didn't poop out in the middle of the night, I plugged it into a power adapter.

Hotel TV + iPod = Entertainment

When I pack for a trip, I take not only my iPod, but an iPod AV composite cable too. Convenient though it may be to watch movies on my iPod while I'm on the plane, when I finally get where I'm going, I want to watch my movies and TV shows on a bigger screen. Every TV in the world has a composite video input—even the ones you find in hotels and motels.

Laptop + iPod = Entertainment

Suppose that you get roped into going to one of those romantic-getaway places that doesn't have a TV. (Shocking, I know, but I hear that there are such places.) If you can sneak your laptop along, just plug your iPod into it, using the included USB cable. Then do this:

1. When the iPod is mounted in iTunes, select it, and enable the Manually Manage Music and Videos option.

2. Click the triangle next to the iPod's name in the Source list and then select Movies or TV Shows.

   The movies or TV shows on your iPod appear in iTunes.

3. Double-click one, and you'll discover that you can play it on your laptop's screen.

4. Choose View > Full Screen to expand the video to take up the entire screen.

Why not just store the videos on your laptop in the first place? Laptop drives don't always have a lot of room to spare. That 160 GB iPod classic, on the other hand, was meant for nothing but media. Put its hard drive to good use.

tip   **This tip works for audio too. If your laptop has a decent set of speakers, play music from your iPod through those speakers. Instant boombox!**

9

Troubleshooting

I regret to report that—except for you, dear reader, and me—nothing is perfect. No, not even the iPod. Whereas it may tick happily along one day, the next day, its menu structure is a mess; it refuses to start up when you're sure it has a full battery; or when it does start up, it displays an icon indicating that it's feeling far from well. In this chapter, I look at the common maladies that afflict the iPod and what, if anything, you can do about them.

iPod Problems and Solutions

Unlike a computer, which can fail in seemingly countless and creative ways, the iPod exhibits only a few behaviors when it's feeling poorly. Following are the most common problems and (when available) their solutions.

Failure to boot

There are a few possible reasons why an iPod may not boot beyond the Apple logo, some benign and others not so:

- **Engaged hold switch.** Go ahead and smack yourself in the head (and then breathe a sigh of relief) if your iPod won't start up because the hold switch is on.

- **Drained battery.** Among the most benign problems is an iPod battery that's drained. If the iPod is functioning normally otherwise, switching it on when its battery is very nearly drained causes a low-battery icon to appear on the display. If the battery is completely drained, the iPod can't even muster the energy to display this icon; the screen remains black. Plug your iPod into a power adapter or your computer, and let it charge. If everything's hunky-dory after that, pat yourself on the back for a job well done.

> **tip** In some rare cases, the battery may not be charged enough for the iPod to be reset. If you've tried other solutions and failed, unplug the iPod from a power supply for 24 hours; then plug it into a power source and attempt to reset it.

- **No charge going to iPod.** If you've plugged the iPod's data/power cable into a computer that isn't currently charging it—one that's turned off or asleep, for example—unplug the iPod. Some people have reported that when the iPod is plugged in but isn't being charged, its power can dissipate quickly.

■ **Computer port problems.** If your computer won't charge your iPod, something may be wrong with its USB port or (in the case of very old iPods) its FireWire port. Try plugging your iPod into a different port or power adapter. If the iPod charges, it's time to cock a suspicious eyebrow at your computer.

Secret Button Combinations

By pressing the proper combination of buttons on the iPod's face, you can force the device to reset, enter Disk Mode, scan its hard disk for damage, and perform a series of diagnostic tests. Here are those combinations and the wonders they perform.

RESET

Resetting the iPod is very much like switching your computer on and off with its power switch. You do this when the iPod is unresponsive—when pressing buttons does nothing, for example. This reset sequence is also the first thing you do before you use other button combinations to engage other hidden actions. To enter Disk Mode, you first reset and then press the Disk Mode button combination (described below).

First three generations of white iPods: Plug the iPod into a powered FireWire device (the Apple iPod Power Adapter, an auto adapter, or a built-in FireWire port); then press and hold the Play and Menu buttons for 6 seconds.

Click-wheel iPods: Plug the iPod into a powered device (the Apple iPod Power Adapter, an auto adapter, or a powered USB port); then press and hold the Center and Menu buttons for 6 seconds.

iPod shuffle: Disconnect the shuffle from your computer, move the toggle switch on the back to the Off position, wait 5 seconds, and

(continued on next page)

Secret Button Combinations (continued)

switch it back to either the Play in Order or Shuffle position. (Yes, resetting a shuffle is really nothing more than turning it off and on again.)

When you reset your iPod, your data remains intact, but the iPod restores the factory settings. This technique reboots the iPod and is helpful when your iPod is locked up.

DISK MODE

Disk Mode is your way to tell the iPod, "Look, I understand you're unhappy, but I need you to mount so that iTunes can see you. When it can, I can restore you and bring you back to full health." This mode forces the iPod to mount.

First three generations of white iPods: Reset the iPod. At the Apple logo, press and hold the Previous and Next buttons.

Click-wheel iPods: Reset the iPod. At the Apple logo, press and hold the Center and Play buttons.

DISK SCAN

First three generations of white iPods: Reset the iPod. At the Apple logo, press and hold Previous, Next, Center, and Menu. An animated icon of a disk and magnifying glass with a progress bar below it appears.

Click-wheel iPods: These iPods don't offer a button combination to scan the hard drive. Rather, you must access this function through the iPod's Diagnostic screen (which I explain at great length later in this chapter).

Use this combination when you want to check the integrity of the iPod's hard drive. This test can take 15 to 20 minutes, so be patient.

Secret Button Combinations (continued)

Be sure to plug your iPod into the power adapter when you perform this test so that the iPod doesn't run out of juice before the scan is complete. If the scan shows no problems, a check mark appears over the disk icon on the first three generations of white iPods.

DIAGNOSTIC MODE

First three generations of white iPods: Reset the iPod. At the Apple logo, press and hold Previous, Next, and Center.

Click-wheel iPods: Reset the iPod. At the Apple logo, press and hold Center and Previous.

See the "Doing Diagnostics" sidebar later in this chapter for more details.

Skipping during playback

Songs played on the iPod may skip for several reasons, including these:

- **Large files.** Large song files (long symphonic movements or those endless Grateful Dead jams, for example) don't play particularly well with the 32 MB RAM buffer on some iPods with hard drives. (Recent high-capacity iPods have a larger RAM buffer and do better with long files.) Large song files race through the RAM buffer, requiring the iPod to access the hard drive more often. This situation can lead to skipping if the iPod is pulling the song almost directly from the hard drive. If possible, reduce the sizes of files by employing greater compression, or chop really long files (such as audiobooks) into pieces.

- **Damaged files.** A damaged song file may skip. If you find that the same song skips every time you play it—and other songs seem to play back with no problem—go back to the source of the song (an audio

CD, for example), rip the song again, and replace the copy on the iPod with the newly ripped version.

- **iPod that needs to be reset.** Yes, an iPod that needs to be reset may cause songs to skip. For an iPod shuffle, a reset entails simply switching the iPod off for 5 seconds. For a click-wheel iPod, hold down the Center and Menu buttons for 6 seconds. If you have a 1G, 2G, or 3G iPod, plug it into a power outlet, and hold down the Play and Menu buttons for 6 seconds.

- **iPod that needs to be restored.** If a reset won't do the trick, make sure that all the data on your iPod is backed up, and restore the iPod from the iPod pane's Summary tab.

The frozen iPod

Just like a computer, the iPod can freeze from time to time. To thaw it, attach your iPod to a power source—a power adapter, a powered FireWire port (for 3G and earlier iPods), or a computer's high-powered USB 2.0 port—and, on the first three generations of the iPod, hold down the Play and Menu buttons for 6 seconds. For click-wheel iPods, hold down the Center and Menu buttons for the same 6 seconds.

Failure to charge

An iPod may not charge for several reasons, including all of the following:

- **Sleeping computer.** The iPod may not charge when it's attached to a sleeping computer. (Some sleeping computers will charge an iPod; others won't.) If you suspect that a sleepy computer is the problem, wake up your computer if you want the iPod to charge.

- **Frozen iPod.** An iPod that's frozen (see the preceding section) won't charge. Reset it.

- **Faulty cable.** Cables break. Try a different data/power cable, just in case yours has gone the way of the dodo.

Doing Diagnostics

Ever wonder what Apple technicians do when they want to test an iPod? Just as you can, they reset the iPod, and when they see the Apple logo, they press and hold Previous, Next, and Center on the first three generations of white iPods, or Center and Previous on click-wheel iPods. When this happens, the screen flashes briefly and then lists a series of tests.

Most of these tests take a gander at the iPod's controllers and internal components—the hard drive or flash memory, display, SDRAM chip, battery, click wheel, and headphone and Dock-connector ports. For most people, these tests are nothing more than a curiosity, which is one reason why Apple refuses to talk about the Diagnostic screen.

For owners of click-wheel iPods, however, these tests can be helpful. Specifically, the tests that scan the hard drive (iPod classics) can go a long way toward telling you whether your iPod's hard drive is on the way out. How you access the hard-drive test depends on which iPod model you have.

On an iPod classic, the first screen will list Manual Test and Auto Test. Press the Menu button to enter Manual Test. Press the Next button to move to IO, and press the Center button. Press Next in the resulting screen to move to the HardDrive entry, and press Center. Select HDSMARTData, and press Center one more time. The screen that appears provides a lot of information about the hard drive. If the Reallocs entry says something other than 0 (particularly something a lot higher than 0), you may have some bad sectors on the drive, which could cause problems for your iPod.

On an iPod nano, you can check memory by entering Diagnostic mode as described, using the Next button to click down to the Memory entry, pressing Center, selecting SDRamoScan, and pressing Center. If everything's going well, you'll see *pass!*

(continued on next page)

> ## Doing Diagnostics (continued)
>
> You're welcome to play with the other tests, if you like. Doing so
> won't hurt the iPod, and perhaps it will help you diagnose a head-
> phone port that doesn't make noise or a click wheel that's occasion-
> ally unresponsive.
>
> To exit Diagnostic mode and restart your iPod, press and hold Center
> and Menu for 6 seconds.

- **Faulty iPod data/power port.** This problem is more common on 1G and 2G iPods than it is on later iPods. As you plug and unplug the FireWire cable from the iPod's FireWire port on these old iPods, it's possible to put too much stress on the internal connectors that deliver power to the port, breaking the bond between those connectors and your iPod's motherboard.

- **Dead battery.** Like all lithium-ion batteries, the iPod's battery is good for 400 to 500 full charges. When you've exhausted those charges, your iPod needs a new battery. See the sidebar "Assault on Batteries" later in this chapter for more details.

- **Broken iPod.** iPods occasionally break (see the following section). If none of these solutions brings your iPod back from its never-ending slumber, it may need to be replaced. Contact Apple at https://selfsolve. apple.com.

The broken iPod

An iPod is a machine, and regrettably, machines break. If none of these solutions brings your iPod back from the dead, it may need to be repaired. If you live near an Apple Store or another outfit that sells iPods, take it in. If such a trip is impractical, contact Apple at https://selfsolve. apple.com for instructions on how to have your iPod serviced.

Assault on Batteries

Nearly all iPods carry a lithium-ion (Li-ion) battery of some sort. Recent iPods hold a lithium-ion polymer battery, which holds a greater number of charges than the original Li-ion type does. Theoretically, the original Li-ion batteries, by their very nature, can be fully charged up to 500 times; in actual practice, your iPod's battery will put up with between 400 and 450 complete charges before it gives up the ghost. A lithium-ion polymer battery drops to 80 percent of its rated capacity after around 400 charges.

This is all well and good if you charge your iPod once a week or so. But if you use your iPod constantly—and, thus, fully charge it four or five times a week—you'll discover that after a couple of years, it's kaput.

If your click-wheel iPod is more than a year old and fails to hold a charge, Apple will replace it with another "functionally equivalent new, used, or refurbished iPod" for $59 (plus $6.95 for shipping). That "functionally equivalent" stuff means that you won't get back the same iPod that you send in. You'll get one from the "good pile" that has the same capacity and is of the same generation as the one you sent in.

If you're mechanically inclined, replacing the battery in a 1G or 2G iPod is fairly easy. A search-engine search will turn up any number of companies willing to sell you a replacement iPod battery, plus the tools and instructions necessary to open the iPod. But newer models are tougher nuts to crack and can be easily broken. For this reason, it's safest to have a professional install your new battery. iResQ (www.iresq.com), Other World Computing (http://eshop. macsales.com), and other companies you can find via a Web search will install a new battery for you.

When you take a misbehaving iPod to a Genius at the Apple Store, said Genius will run a couple of tests on it. If the iPod fails to respond, the Genius may try to restore it (which is why you should always have a backup of your music and data).

If that doesn't work, and your iPod is under warranty, you'll probably get a replacement on the spot (provided that Apple still sells the same iPod model, with the same storage capacity, as the one you bring in). If Apple has changed the iPod line—you've got a 3G iPod nano, for example, and Apple now sells the 5G iPod nano—according to Apple, your iPod "will be replaced with functionally equivalent new, used, or refurbished iPod equipment." In other words, you *may* get the new model, but if there's an available refurbished version of the iPod you bring in, you'll likely get it. If the iPod is out of warranty, you'll have to pay for the repair.

iTunes Problems and Solutions

Given the number of tasks that iTunes is tasked with, it's remarkable that it works at all. Yet most of the time, it does and does so flawlessly. When it doesn't, there's often a simple fix that will put things right.

The dreaded gray question mark of confusion

You launch iTunes, click a track, and attempt to play it. Instead of the lilting (or hammering, I suppose) sound you expected, you get a gray question mark next to the track's name—the iTunes equivalent of "Huh?!?"

The question mark indicates that iTunes can't find the track you'd like to play. In all likelihood, if you attempt to play other tracks in your iTunes Library, you'll see more of this terse punctuation. If you do, you will because you've unmounted the drive that contains your iTunes Library or moved the folder where the track once lived, or because the track has been vaporized in some way.

First, open iTunes' Preferences, click the Advanced tab, and check the iTunes Media folder location. Is it pointing where you expect it to—to an external drive where you moved your iTunes Library? If not, and if iTunes has reverted to the default location for the iTunes Music folder (within your Music or My Music folder), the drive that holds your music has gone missing. Mount it and restart iTunes, and all should be well.

If the location is correct, and the drive and folder are where they should be, search for the track. Did something happen to it? If it's indeed missing, use your computer's Search function to look for it. Return it to its original location or drag it into your iTunes Library.

Dealing with duplicates

Over time, it's possible—even likely—that your iTunes Library will be crammed with duplicate files. Yet weeding out duplicates can be a chore. iTunes offers a rather broad way of dealing with them: Just choose File > Show Duplicates. The iTunes window will display a list of files that it believes are duplicates.

Before you start trashing these "duplicate" files, however, check the albums they come from, and compare their times. iTunes checks only track title and artist when it checks for duplicates. If you have both the studio and live versions of a track, iTunes may deem them duplicates.

Because iTunes isn't terribly discerning about duplicates, if you have a serious duplicates problem, turn to a third-party tool. For Windows users, one of those tools is MarkelSoft's $35 Dupe Eliminator for iTunes (www.markelsoft.com). Mac users get a better deal with Lairware's $20 Song Sergeant (www.lairware.com) or Doug Adams' $15 Dupin (http://dougscripts.com). All of these utilities use far more exacting filtering than iTunes does; thus, they're better at identifying duplicate files. They also provide ways to select and remove those duplicate files.

Files misfiled

If you followed some of my tips in Chapter 8 for moving videos into your iTunes Library, you may find that they aren't filed where they should be. TV shows are listed under the Movies heading, for example, and audiobooks make their presence known in the Music area. The secret to filing these things correctly is the Options tab within an item's Info window. To put things right, do this:

1. Select the misfiled items, and choose File > Get Info.

2. In the window that appears, click the Options tab.

3. From the Media Kind pop-up menu, choose the kind of media you have: Music Video, Movie, TV Show, Video Podcast, or iTunes U for video files, or Music, Podcast, iTunes U, Audiobook, or Voice Memo for audio files.

4. Click OK.

   The file you were working on will be filed correctly.

note You can do this with multiple files—a series of audiobook chapters, for example. Just select all the files that you'd like to change, choose File > Get Info, confirm that you really do want to work on multiple files, click the Options tab in the window that appears, choose the media type from the pop-up menu, and click OK.

Sluggish iTunes

If iTunes is slow to start up or slow to respond when it's running, one of these fixes may help.

Where's your iTunes Library?

If you have the contents of your iTunes Library scattered across multiple drives or on an external drive that has to spin up before iTunes will run at its best, it may take a while for iTunes to get its house in order. You can put up with that behavior, or you might consider consolidating your library so that everything is on a single drive—one that doesn't have to spin up. Look in Chapter 8 to learn how to consolidate your library.

tip **Also pay attention to the Home Sharing discussion in Chapter 8. Home Sharing lets you gather together all the media you have scattered on two or more computers.**

Launch in Safe Mode

You can launch iTunes 9 so that visual plug-ins are disabled. Older plug-ins used with a new version of iTunes can cause problems; disabling them gives you an idea of whether a plug-in is an issue.

To launch in Safe Mode on a Mac, hold down Command and Option while launching iTunes. On a Windows PC, press Shift+Ctrl and launch the program. You'll see a dialog box telling you that you've launched into Safe Mode.

If third-party plug-ins appear to be the problem (those from Apple should be OK), you can remove them manually. On a Mac, you'll find them by following this path: *user folder*/Library/iTunes/iTunes Plug-Ins. On a Windows PC, they'll be in Program Files/iTunes.

Index